John Cordy Jeaffreson, Christopher Jeaffreson

A Young Squire of the Seventeenth Century From the Papers (A.D. 1676-1686)

Vol. I

John Cordy Jeaffreson, Christopher Jeaffreson

A Young Squire of the Seventeenth Century From the Papers (A.D. 1676-1686)
Vol. I

ISBN/EAN: 9783337025250

Printed in Europe, USA, Canada, Australia, Japan

Cover: Foto ©ninafisch / pixelio.de

More available books at **www.hansebooks.com**

A YOUNG SQUIRE

OF THE

SEVENTEENTH CENTURY.

—

VOL. I.

A YOUNG SQUIRE

OF THE

SEVENTEENTH CENTURY.

FROM THE PAPERS (A.D. 1676-1686)

OF

CHRISTOPHER JEAFFRESON,

OF DULLINGHAM HOUSE, CAMBRIDGESHIRE.

EDITED BY

JOHN CORDY JEAFFRESON,

AUTHOR OF

"A BOOK ABOUT DOCTORS," "BRIDES AND BRIDALS," ETC.

IN TWO VOLUMES.
VOL. I.

LONDON:
HURST AND BLACKETT, PUBLISHERS,
13, GREAT MARLBOROUGH STREET.
1878.

CONTENTS

OF

THE FIRST VOLUME.

Part I.

A BIOGRAPHICAL AND HISTORICAL MEMOIR.

CHAPTER I.
EXPLORERS AND PLANTERS.

Birth and Parentage of the Letter-Writer—His Father's Birth and Boyhood—Three Suffolk Lads—Woodbridge Port—Mariners of Western England—Sailors of East Anglia—Roger North—Thomas Warner—John Winthrop of Groton—The American Dialect . . 3

CHAPTER II.
THE THREE PARTNERS.

Captain Thomas Painton—His great Notion about Plantations—Ralphe Merifield, the London Merchant—Warner's Expedition—His Comrades—The first English Settlement of St. Christopher's Island—'The Hopewell'—

James Hay, Earl of Carlisle—Charles the First's Commission to Thomas Warner and John Jeaffreson—The same King's Grant to the Earl of Carlisle—Emigrants from Suffolk to the West Indies—Disputes between the Earls of Carlisle and Marlborough—The First English Colony in the West Indies 14

CHAPTER III.

THE PERILS OF PLANTING.

The Stream of Emigrants from England to the West Indies—Warner's Visits to England—His Character—Jealousy of France and Spain—Dangers surrounding the West Indian Planter—Spanish Insolence and Cruelty.—The Duke of Lerma and Don Lewis Firardo—Spanish Atrocities at Tortuga—The Massacre at Santa Cruz—Cromwell's Vengeance on Spain—Slaughter of the Caribees and their Expulsion from St. Christopher's Island—The Bucaneers—Their Character and Pursuits . 31

CHAPTER IV.

THE TWO NATIONS.

The Various Nationalities of the European Settlements in the West Indies—Incessant Conflicts of the Plantations—Their Participation in the Civil Commotions of the European States—West Indian Planters punished for their Loyalty to Charles the First and Charles the Second—Punished in the next Generation for adhering to William the Third—Origin of the French Colony on St. Christopher's Island—Sir Thomas Warner's Reasons for allowing the French to settle there—Mutual Jealousies and Animosities of the two Settlements—Successive Wars between the French and English on St. Christopher's Island 45

CONTENTS. vii

CHAPTER V.

A FORTUNATE ADVENTURER.

The Colonel's Retirement from St. Christopher's Island—His Services to the English Colony there—Conquest of the Island by Don Frederick of Toledo—The Colonel's Marriage—He commands a Ship in the Anglo-Dutch Naval Battle of 1653—His Wealth—His Death and Disposal of his Estates—The Letter-Writer's Education 54

CHAPTER VI.

FROM LONDON TO THE LEEWARD ISLANDS.

The Letter-Writer's Early Marriage—Death of his Bride—He determines to make the Voyage to St. Christopher's Island—Reasons for this Determination—His Departure from Billingsgate—Incidents of the Voyage—His Sojourn at Madeira—His Stay at Mountserrat—His Shorter Stay at Nevis—His Arrival at St. Christopher's Island 63

CHAPTER VII.

IN WHICH THE LETTER-WRITER FIGURES AS STORE-KEEPER, PLANTER, AND MEMBER OF PARLIAMENT.

Christopher's Store—The Poverty of his Island—Trade without Money—Current Value of Sugar and Indigo—Freights of Merchant-Adventurers from London to the West Indies—Goods sold at the Store—Dearth of Labour in the Colony—Wages of skilled and common Workmen —Emigrants reluctant to settle in the West Indian Islands—Honest but poor Mr. Worley—His neglect of the Letter-Writer's Property—Christopher resolves to turn Planter—His Difficulty in ascertaining the Boundaries and Titles of his Properties—He becomes a Member of the Colonial Assembly—The Arrogance of the French Colony—Mutual Animosities of the two Nations—The Battle between the French and Dutch at Tobago . 73

CHAPTER VIII.

UNDER ARMS.

Ensign Thorn of the St. Kitt's Militia—His Endowments and Chief Ambition--West Indian Stewards for Absentee Proprietors—A Short Life and a Merry One—West Indian Morality—Edward Thorn on his Good Behaviour —His Mission to London and his Victims there—A Man of Straw passing for a Man of Capital—An Alarm of War between England and France—War Panic in the Leeward Islands—In Garrison and on Guard—The French Fleet reinforced by Bucaneers—The Alarm at Nevis— Departure of the Fleet and Subsidence of the Panic— Hurtful Consequences of the Alarm—Bad News from England—The Store at Wingfield Manor . . 90

CHAPTER IX.

CHRISTOPHER'S FOURTH YEAR IN THE WEST INDIES.

Depression of Agriculture—Dullness of Trade—Financial Trouble at Boston—The Proposal to appoint Colonel Gamiell to be London Agent for the Colony—The Treaty of Neutrality—The Letter-Writer's part in the Negotiations for the Treaty—Renewal of Alarms—The French Admiral D'Estrées courting the Bucaneers—French Insolence and Outrages—Failure of the Negotiations for the Treaty of Neutrality—Christopher's Store and his Venture in Horse-flesh—The Gallants of St. Kitt's . 103

CHAPTER X.

IN LOVE.

Christopher's serious Illness—Mortality of his Slaves—His Anxiety caused by Edward Thorn's Absence—The Agent's Return with a Cargo of Horses and Mares—The Letter-Writer recovers his Health and Spirits—Alarming Illness of Governor Matthews—The Princess of Nevis—Her Age and Fortune—Christopher is advised to make her an Offer of Marriage—His Friendly Relations with the Young Lady's Kindred—Value of Money in the days of the Stuarts—Christopher consents to accompany Colonel Matthews to England—The Colonel's Death—A Change of Plan 110

CHAPTER XI.

CHRISTOPHER'S LAST YEAR IN THE COLONY.

New Clothes—Rejected Addresses—The Great Hurricane—The Second Tempest—The Letter-Writer's Resolution to "go home"—He appoints Edward Thorn to take charge of his Plantations—A Colonial Farewell—The Captain-General confers with him on Matters of Public Interest—Sir William Stapleton entrusts him with Commissions to be executed in London—Homeward Bound—Arrival in London 118

CHAPTER XII.

CHANNELL ROW, WESTMINSTER.

Charles Brett's Death—His Parentage and Office at Court—His Interment and Mural Tablet in St. Margaret's Church, Westminster—The Name and Neighbourhood of Channell Row—The Letter-Writer's London Address—

Tokens and Token-Drinking—The Token-Feast at the Sun Tavern—Constantine Phipps of Gray's Inn—Edward Thorn Unmasked—His Profligate Life in St. Christopher's Island—Colonial Morality. . . . 125

CHAPTER XIII.

A COLONIAL COMMISSIONER IN DIFFICULTIES.

Failures in Lombard Street—Panic in the City—The Fall of Bantam—The Rye House Plot—Mr. Blathwait's Services—Christopher's Petition to the King and Council for Soldiers—His Petition for Military Munitions—Success in the Council Chamber—Failure in the Department—Lord Dartmouth's Significant Speech—Christopher's Petition for an Allotment of Malefactors—Order of the Council respecting the same Petition—Corrupt Practices of the Gaoler of Newgate and the Recorder of London—Futile Contention with those Officers—Mr. Blathwait's Advice—Sir Leoline Jenkins's Intervention—Christopher's Speech to the Lords of the Council—His Defeat. . . , . . . 138

CHAPTER XIV.

ANOTHER YEAR OF SERVICE.

The hard Winter of 1683-4—Frost Fair—Prevalence of Small Pox—Death Rate of the Capital—"Mourning" the Fashionable Dress—Deaths of Sir Edward Brett and Colonel Gamiell—Intrigues and Competitors for Sir William Stapleton's Office—Christopher's exertions for his Colony—His First Shipment of Malefactors to St. Christopher's Island—He is appointed London Agent for his Colony—He presents Addresses to the King and the Duke of York on their Preservation from the Rye House Conspiracy—His Second Marriage—He moves from Channell Row to Cornhill . . . 148

CHAPTER XV.
THE LAST OF THE MEMOIR.

Charles the Second's Death—James the Second's Accession—Argyll's Insurrection—French Refugees—The last Year's Letters—How they should be read—Notable Scenes—The Malefactors' March—Governor Hill's Breach of Contract—How Mr. Vickers kept his Word—American Smartness—West Indian Morality . 154

Part II.

THE VOYAGE TO THE WEST INDIES AND THE LETTERS FROM ST. CHRISTOPHER'S ISLAND.

CHAPTER I.
OUTWARD BOUND.

(16 *Feb.* 167$\frac{5}{6}$ *to* 24 *May*, 1676.)

The Writer's Desire to visit St. Christopher's Island—He takes Leave of his Friends in Billingsgate—Gravesend— Margaret Road — Plymouth—Catwater — Windbound Ships—The Deserts Islands—Madeira—Funchial —Curious Superstitions and Religious Usages—The Enchanted Island—The Canary Islands—Flying Fish, Dolphins and Bunnitoes—A Gale—Descade, Guadaloupe and Antigua—Hospitable Entertainment at Mountserrat —Nevis—St. Christopher's Island . . . 167

CHAPTER II.

THE FIRST YEAR IN ST. CHRISTOPHER'S ISLAND.

(24 May 1676 to 11 November 1676.)

A West-Indian ' Store'—Trade in the Leeward Islands—The Islanders' favourite Wine—Want of Artisans—'Honest' Mr. Worley—Indigo and Sugar—The Writer turns Planter—Apprehensions of War—Poverty of the Planters—Goods most needed by them—The Writer's Sugar-Work—A West-Indian Agent in London—French Planters—Their Jealousy and Insolence—Lady Stapleton—Sir William Stapleton, Captain-General of the 'Leeward Islands'—Extent and Boundaries of the Writer's Plantations 182

CHAPTER III.

THE CONTINUATION OF THE FIRST YEAR IN ST. CHRISTOPHER'S ISLAND.

(11 November, 1676, to 24 May, 1677.)

Rival Colonies—Proposed Treaty of Neutrality—Current Values of Sugar and Indigo—Currency—Wages—Agriculture—English Military Force in St. Christopher's Island—French Predominance—Fight between the French and Dutch at Tobago—The Two Nations—Dutch Privateers—Destructiveness of War in the West Indies—Trade of St. Christopher's Island—Shipping at Nevis—Lockier's Pills. 203

CHAPTER IV.

THE SECOND AND THIRD YEARS IN ST. CHRISTOPHER'S ISLAND.

(24 May, 1677, to 24 May, 1679.)

Edward Thorn in England—Apprehensions of War—West Indian Rumours of War between England and France—Panic in St. Christopher's Island—Colonists in Arms—Count d'Estrées and his Fleet—A Bucaneer Fleet of Thirty Sail—A Fleet of Merchantmen—The Alarm at Nevis—Withdrawal of the Fleets—A Suit in Chancery—Ventures in the West Indies—Success in Commerce—Expenditure on Planting—Goods sent out from England—A Salesman on Commission—Colonial Needs . 219

CHAPTER V.

THE FOURTH YEAR IN ST. CHRISTOPHER'S ISLAND.

(24 May, 1679, to 24 May, 1680.)

Colonial Agents in London—The English Colonists of St Kitts require a new London Agent—The Agency offered to Colonel Gamiell—French Insolence and Discourtesy—Assassination of an English Soldier—Slaves landed at Nevis—A great Fire at Boston—Commercial Dullness in New England—William Calhoun—Colonel Matthews—Sir William Stapleton and the Count de Blanarque—Futile Negotiations for an Anglo-French Treaty of Neutrality—The Gallants of the Leeward Islands—Ventures in New England. 237

CHAPTER VI.

THE FIFTH YEAR IN ST. CHRISTOPHER'S ISLAND.

(24 May, 1680, to 24 May, 1681.)

Intrigues for the Agency—The Writer in Trouble—Edward Thorn's Absence and Reappearance—Scarcity of Artisans and White Labourers—Prospects of Emigrants—West-Indian Adventurers—The Writer in Love—Mistress Frances Russell's Age and Fortune—A Christening at Government House, Nevis—Death of Colonel Matthews—The Writer's Perplexities—His Resolve to spend another Year in the West Indies—Affairs at Dullingham 251

CHAPTER VII.

THE SIXTH AND LAST YEAR IN ST. CHRISTOPHER'S ISLAND.

(24 May, 1681, to 24 May, 1682.)

Brave Clothing—Rejected Addresses—A strenuous Suit and baffled Suitor—Hurricanes in St. Christopher's Island—Injuries done to the Writer's House and Plantations—Sufferings inflicted by the Storms on the Writer's Slaves—His Exertions in their Behalf—Horses imported from New England—Aunt Peacock's Curiosity touching Mistress Frances Russell — Charles Brett's Good Services 267

CHAPTER VIII.

HOMEWARD BOUND.

(12 July, 1682, to 17 September, 1682.)

The 'St. Nicolas'—Tediousness of the Voyage—Mishaps in a Gale—The Writer's Accounts—Orders to his Agent and Steward—Ensign Edward Thorn—The Writer's Consideration for his Negroes and White Servants—List of his Friends in St. Christopher's Island—Their flattering Farewell to him on his Departure for England—Westcoat Bay near Margate—Off Dover—Entertainment on Board Ship—The French Success at Algiers . 282

Part III.

LONDON LETTERS.

CHAPTER I.

OLD FRIENDS AND NEW FACES.

(17 September, 1682, to 17 October, 1682.)

London Friends—Charles Brett's Death—Mr. Penney, the London Tailor—Mrs. Penney's Revelations touching Edward Thorn—The Young Man's Victims and Knavish Tricks—Troubles of the Kidnabbers — Captain Hill—Postponement of Journeys to Cambridgeshire, Suffolk and Buckinghamshire—Aunt Parkyns's Prayers—Governor Hill's Petition for a Loan of the Writer's House in St. Christopher's Island 293

CHAPTER II.

FRIENDLY GREETINGS AND FIRST MEETINGS.

(17 October, 1682, to 17 November, 1682.)

James Phipps's Ill Health—Token-Drinking at 'The Sun' —A Family Party—Constantine Phipps and the Gray's Inn Revels—Edward Thorn's crafty Proposal—Severe

Handling of the Kidnabbers—Consequent Alarm of West-Indian Merchants—The Writer's Petition for a Grant of Malefactors—Mr. Blathwait—Governor Hill—His Dependence on Sir William Stapleton—John Beddinfield's Death—Tokens from a Father in the West Indies to his Sons in London—Official Men and Manners—The Writer acting for the Captain-General—Information and Gossip for His Excellency . . . 309

INTRODUCTION.

THE documents, published in these volumes, were written between February, 1676 and September, 1686, by an English gentleman of good education and estate, who, on the completion of his twenty-second year, came into possession of important properties in Suffolk and Cambridgeshire, as well as large plantations in St. Christopher's Island, in the West Indies.

In his twenty-seventh year, he made the voyage to St. Kitt's, in order that he might settle and restore his estate in that island. Having left England with the intention of spending from fifteen to twenty-four months at sea and in foreign parts, he passed five years in the West Indies, where he worked energetically as a planter and merchant, and took an active part in the political affairs of his colony. Returning to England in his thirty-second year, he resided four years in London, acting as political agent for Sir William Stapleton, Bart., the Captain-general of the Leeward Islands, and as Commissioner of the English Colony of St. Kitt's.

The Letters, written by his hand during his residence in St. Kitt's, afford an equally comprehensive and minute account of the constitution, tone and circumstances of West Indian society in Charles the Second's time.

The one hundred and fifty-four Letters, written from London (for the greater part to residents in the Leeward Islands) are even more entertaining; for, whilst they abound with particulars that complete the previous sketches of colonial life, they tell with singular vividness the political and social story of London, during four unusually stirring and eventful years. Whilst some of these epistles were written at the instigation of affection, or from mere social kindliness, others were penned for the furtherance of the writer's private affairs. But the majority of the Letters were written, in the way of official service, for the enlightenment of the Captain-general of the Leeward Islands, the Governor of St. Kitt's, and other chief residents in the writer's colony. The writer was, in fact, one of the Special and Private Correspondents, who, in the infancy of journalism, furnished their friends, in places remote from England, with the latest London news on matters about which the meagre Gazettes and Intelligencers were imperfectly communicative, or altogether silent. Exhibiting with picturesque brightness the amusements and trivial excitements of London society, they afford many notable particulars of European politics and movements, and contain a series of careful accounts of momentous occurrences.

The papers have several distinct claims to attention. They are rich in facts for those who, taking an especial interest in the colonial enterprise of the present century, desire a larger knowledge of our colonizing activity in previous times. They are still richer in illustrations of the social life of the English in Restoration England. The narrative of the writer's adventures equals, in succession of excitements and variety of incidents, the best realistic tales of adventure. The writer will also be studied with curiosity and gratification as a type of a particular class of young Englishmen, who have received no sufficient attention from historians of their period.

Popular history has taught us to divide the young squires of Restoration England into two classes—the sottish fox-hunters, who lived almost entirely in the country, and the swaggering gallants, who squandered their substance in the taverns and theatres of London. The prominence given to these two species of English gentlemen is apt to make us forgetful of the numerous class of landed proprietors, who, enjoying the chase with moderation, and society without abandonment, were alike innocent of rural loutishness and urbane profligacy. The letter-writer belonged to the squires of this last-named kind. A gentleman of sobriety and intelligence, he attended the Newmarket Meetings, but avoided the company and vices of gamblers. With no ambition to figure as a wit, or man of pleasure, he took a healthy delight in gaiety and diversions. Prosperity endowed him with no disposition to shirk his social obligations. Courteous and unaffected, he made his place and kept it amongst men of his degree, by energy and good sense, rather than by brilliant parts.

During the years covered by the documents, it was his practice to preserve copies of his more important letters in the folio Letter-Book, which has afforded the materials for the present work. This MS. volume is in good condition, though the ink of some of the writing has faded. Some of the copies were made by servants; but the majority of the transcripts, like the original manuscript of the " The Voyage of St. Christopher," were entered into the ledger by the letter-writer himself. The occasional inconsistencies of spelling, observable in the transcripts, may in some cases be attributed to the carelessness of clerks, who were at no pains to copy with literal accuracy.

J. C. J.

Part I.

A BIOGRAPHICAL AND HISTORICAL
MEMOIR.

CHAPTER I.

EXPLORERS AND PLANTERS.

Birth and Parentage of the Letter-Writer—His Father's Birth and Boyhood—Three Suffolk Lads—Woodbridge Port—Mariners of Western England—Sailors of East Anglia—Roger North—Thomas Warner—John Winthrop of Groton—The American Dialect.

BORN in 1650, the writer of the letters, edited in these volumes, was in his seventy-fifth year when he died at Dullingham House, Cambridgeshire, in the year 1725. His monument in Dullingham Church bears the following inscription :—

"Near this place lyes interred, in hopes of a blessed resurrection, ye body of Christopher Jeaffreson of this county, Esqre., and son of Colonell John Jeaffreson, of St. Andrews, Holbourn, in ye county of Middlesex, and of

Mary his wife, Daughter of Aden Parkins, Esqre., of ye county of Nottingham. He departed this life ye 1st of August, 1725, in ye 75th year of his age. His eminent good qualities were so many, and his Impartiality in Administering Justice in his county so conspicuous, that he died greatly lamented by all who had ye happiness to know him."

Of the Mary Parkins (or Parkyns) mentioned in this epitaph, it is enough to say that she was a Mistress Parkins of Bunney, Co. Nottingham, and first-cousin of Colonel Isham Parkins, who defended Ashby de la Zouche against the Parliament, and spent a considerable fortune in Charles the First's service and cause.

But in order that the reader may fully enjoy the ensuing letters, and regard a past generation from their writer's stand-point, it is necessary to speak more fully of the fortunate adventurer, who is described on his son's tomb-stone as " Colonell John Jeaffreson, of St. Andrew's, Holbourn, in ye County of Middlesex."

The son of a gentle yeoman, whose small

estate lay in the parishes of Petistree and
Clopton, Co. Suffolk, this John Jeaffreson
was born at Petistree within four or five
miles of Parham, where the family of Warner
had resided for several generations on an
estate consisting of a mansion and a few
small farms. The Jeaffresons of Petistree
and the Warners of Parham were on terms
of intimacy; and in their boyhood a close
friendship was formed by John Jeaffreson
and Thomas Warner, who were in future
years so largely instrumental in planting the
West Indies with English colonists. Besides
his particular friend Thomas Warner, this
son of the Petistree yeoman had several
playmates. He had an elder brother, Joseph,
who was content to live and die on his
ancestral acres, and a younger brother,
Samuel, who, on reaching manhood, sailed
westward to share the fortunes of his adventurous brother. He had also several cousins
in his native county, who were induced by
his successful example to throw up their
little farms in East Anglia, and occupy wider
grounds in the islands of the sun.

Born in "the spacious time of great Elizabeth," when the desire for maritime adventure was the prevailing passion of the cadets of gentle houses, who were too poor to live in idleness, and too proud to don the livery of serving-men, each of these three lads—John and Sam Jeaffreson, and Tom Warner—conceived and nursed the ambition to emulate the heroism of Humphry Gilbert and surpass the achievements of Francis Drake. They often visited the small river-port of Woodbridge, where they heard the talk of sea-faring men, who fired their imaginations with stories of the deep. Thirsting for adventure in the New World, they pined for the free open sea, and went to it by the nearest way. Taking ship at Woodbridge, they dropt down the pleasant Deben, and moved over the great waters, on which they were appointed to do much business.

In Transatlantic discovery the mariners of our western ports surpassed the sailors of our eastern havens. Humphry Gilbert, Francis Drake, Walter Raleigh, and John Hawkins were Devonshire men; and no other county of England contributed four such men to the nautical enterprise of the Elizabethan epoch. Suffolk, no doubt, produced Cavendish, who squandered a noble patrimony at Court before he thought of restoring his shattered fortunes by plundering the Spaniard in the Western Seas; and though he was born in Yorkshire, Frobisher, who throughout his maritime career hailed from Harwich, belongs to East Anglia rather than his native county. And other daring explorers of the Elizabethan age started on their westward voyages from our eastern havens. The annals of Yarmouth and Southwold, Aldborough and Ipswich contribute many a bright page to the naval history of Tudor England. But a comparison of our men of the west with our men of the east, who distinguished themselves greatly in Transatlantic adventure during the earlier times of American exploration, would end in favour of the former.

But if the western mariners led the way in exploration and plunder, the eastern adventurers gained the higher honours, and achieved the more enduring results in colonization. The West gave us the brightest specimens of those eminently Elizabethan privateersmen, who combined the characteristics of the pirate and bucaneer with the qualities of the naval officer and the merchant adventurer, and who were animated by appetite for gold and bloodshed quite as much as by love of knowledge and country. But our plantations were, for the most part, given us by men of our eastern shires.

Elizabethan exploration did little for the colonization of the New World. Raleigh's attempts at planting were dismal failures. He gave Virginia her name, but he endowed her with no enduring colony. A similar account must be given of some of our other primitive efforts for the settlement of America. When they did not result in complete failure, they fell far short of imperfect success.

Our ancestors had learnt how much easier it was to seize Spanish galleons than to raise new states; when the influence of a series of remarkable leaders, even more than the irritations of religious persecution, caused the tide of emigration to run for several years strongly and steadily from East Anglia to the Western Indies. Of these leaders, by far the most important were Roger North, a member of a noble East Anglian stock, Thomas Warner, the son of a gentle Suffolk yeoman, and John Winthrop, of Groton, a Suffolk squire.

To these men the work of Anglo-American colonization is mainly referable. North contributed towards the achievement the sanction of his name and the suggestions of a sound and thoroughly practical intellect. Warner and Winthrop were the great leaders, who lured men from the Old to the New World, and planted them in the latter by hundreds and by thousands.

Warner's plantations were made in the islands; but in settling his colonies of St. Christopher's Island, Nevis, and Antigua, he contributed largely to the colonization of the American mainland. Nevis, Antigua, and Mountserrat were not planted till the English colony of St. Christopher's Island suffered from an excess of white population; and eight years before Sir Thomas Warner's death in 1648, the little island of Nevis contained four thousand whites. The redundancy of white population in the insular plantations flowed to the continent. Several of the oldest and best English families of the United States found their way thither by way of the West Indies.

On leaving the shores of Old England, Winthrop made straight for the coasts of New England. His destination was the main-land; and when his fleet of four vessels —the 'Arbella,' the 'Talbot,' the 'Ambrose,' and the 'Jewel'—sailed for Massachusetts, the prevailing dialect of crews and passengers was the distinctive dialect of the Eastern counties.

Of course Warner and Winthrop welcomed followers, from whatever part of the old country they might come; but it may be said of each that a great majority of his companions were natives of East Anglia. The early records of St. Christopher's Island, Nevis, Antigua, and Mountserrat declare this provincial source of our earliest settlements in the Western Indies. In some parts of Norfolk, Suffolk, Essex and Cambridgeshire, John Winthrop's emigration with so large a force of friends, tenants, and religious sympathizers is still called "the Great Exodus." Of the two thousand persons who are computed to have accompanied or shortly followed him to Massachusetts, at least eighteen hundred quitted homes in our Eastern counties; and the arrival of so large a number of East Anglian emigrants in New England, at a time when all the English settlers in the several settlements of the main-land did not exceed a few hundreds, had a permanent effect on the language of the Anglo-American people. It fixed the dialect of the entire community of the continental colonists, who, in consequence of the predominance of the East Anglian element in the insular settlements, already comprised a large proportion of people whose speech exhibited the peculiar and unmistakeable intonations and phrases of Eastern counties' talk.

The predominant dialect of the American Republic—the dialect which strikes the ear far more strongly in the New England than the other States, but may be detected in the common parlance of the entire Union—is the East Anglian dialect; and the American people should be more proud than ashamed of the peculiarity which is the oldest and most English of their institutions. In England it is the fashion to say that the nasal whine of the old Puritans survives in the nasal intonations of their American descendants. And the remark is altogether true, and in no way misleading to those who bear in mind that the seventeenth century Puritans, who fixed the dialect of the American States, spoke with the nasal drant and drawl, and the vocal pitch and fall, not because they were Puritans, but because they were East Anglians.

Should any educated American be disposed to form his own opinion on this alleged resemblance, or rather this alleged identity of the Eastern counties' dialect and the American pronunciation of the English language, let him run down by the Great Eastern Railway from London to "high Suffolk," or spend an afternoon at Woodbridge Market. To ascertain how rich the common speech of the same county is in the so-called Americanisms of expression, he must pass six months in familiar intercourse with the farmers and humbler peasantry of the district.

Whilst surveying the migratory movement of which Warner and Winthrop were the principal leaders, the student does well to be mindful of its effect on the speech of the English Americans of the present generation.

CHAPTER II.

THE THREE PARTNERS.

Captain Thomas Painton—His great Notion about Plantations—Ralphe Merifield, the London Merchant—Warner's Expedition—His Comrades—The first English Settlement of St. Christopher's Island—'The Hopewell'—James Hay, Earl of Carlisle—Charles the First's Commission to Thomas Warner and John Jeaffreson—The same King's Grant to the Earl of Carlisle—Emigrants from Suffolk to the West Indies—Disputes between the Earls of Carlisle and Marlborough—The First English Colony in the West Indies.

THOMAS WARNER was making a voyage to Surinam in company with Captain Roger North, when he had the good fortune to become acquainted with Captain Painton, one of the several experienced seamen who surrounded the mariner of an ennobled name.

These seamen had their special views on questions pertaining to maritime adventure and colonization; and one of Captain Painton's favourite notions was that colonies should be planted on the small islands of the Indian Seas, where the ocean afforded them a natural defence against hostile intruders, and circumscribed the field of uncertain dangers. The opinion was one of those essentially insular sentiments that are natural to the Englishman, who has been trained by circumstances to be thankful for " the strip of blue" that divides him and his people from their natural enemies, the foreigners of the European Continent.

On a small island, Captain Painton used to argue, a young and feeble colony would enjoy a measure of security from a sudden invasion by Indians, which the nature of things denied to settlements on the mainland. A little band of resolute whites could be sure of holding their ground against the natives of a single island. Moreover, the belt of sea might be greatly serviceable to a growing plantation in preserving it from the evil consequences of the sudden and capricious departure of a considerable proportion of its own citizens. Even when it had overcome adverse forces in the first struggles for existence, and was making rapid advances to firm establishment, what should save a plantation, flanked by interminable woods and prairies, from falling to ruin at any moment from the mere restlessness and delight in vagrancy, that actuate so powerfully and irregularly the persons who are capable of deserting civilized societies, in order that they may find homes in desert places.

Thomas Warner was impressed by the reasonableness of these views; and he returned to England in 1620 with the purpose of acting on the suggestions of a fellow-voyager who had already passed to another life. Thomas Painton being no longer alive to give practical effect to his conclusions, Thomas Warner rendered the sincerest homage to the dead man's sagacity by adopting his ideas.

In London he took counsel with Mr. Ralphe Merifield, a merchant who had been caught by the mania for making ventures and founding plantations in the New World. He had recourse also to his old comrade and schoolmate, John Jeaffreson, who had already become an experienced navigator. The result of many interviews and much deliberation was that these three men entered into partnership, and agreed to carry out one of the most notable schemes of emigration that had been laid since the discovery of America.

It was arranged that Thomas Warner should collect a small band of suitable men and take them to Virginia, where they would hire a craft in which to cruise about the Caribeean Seas, and make a choice of islands suited to their project. Having planted himself and comrades on St. Christopher's or some neighbouring island, Warner would dismiss the Virginian craft with instructions that would make known his precise position in the West Indian Archipelago to his confederates in London. In the meantime Mr. Ralphe Merifield would make choice of a suitable vessel, and furnish it in every particular for a voyage across the Atlantic. John Jeaffreson promised to hold himself ready to take command of this vessel and sail westward with a cargo of adventurers, tools and provisions, to his friend's assistance.

Each of the parties to this contract fulfilled his engagement.

Warner displayed his knowledge of character in choosing these fourteen comrades in adventure:—William Tasted, John Rhodes, Robert Binns, Mr. Benifield, Serjeant Jones, Mr. Ware, William Ryle, Rowland Grasscocke, Mr. Bond, Mr. Langley, Mr. Weaver, Serjeant Aplon, a nameless sailor, and an unnamed cook. He was also accompanied by his brave son Edward, then only thirteen years of age, and by his still braver wife. Including Mrs. Warner and her boy, the party numbered just seventeen persons; and for a time they met with unqualified success. Having crossed the Atlantic as passengers in a seaworthy vessel, they landed in Virginia; and they succeeded in finding a skipper to transport them to St. Christopher's Island, where they arrived in January, 1623, and met with a friendly reception from the Caribees. When the Virginian craft set sail for the mainland, Warner and his comrades were busily employed in making huts, and preparing land for the cultivation of corn and tobacco; the corn being sown for the sustenance of the labourers, and the tobacco being planted so that Mr. Ralphe Merifield's ship might have a cargo of " the weed" to carry back to England.

All went well with the adventurers till a late time in 1623, when one of those hurricanes that are apt to occur at a particular season of the year in the West Indies, swept away their flimsy habitations, destroyed their standing corn, and rooting up their tobaccoplants, carried every leaf of them beyond recovery. By this disaster the pioneers were reduced to a deplorable condition. They were without dwellings and without food. For the moment, also, the shock had deprived them of heart and energy to make the best of their miserable circumstances. The Caribees, who had suffered no less severely than the strangers from the violent storm, could do little for the relief and protection of the intruders. For a while it seemed inevitable that the small and luckless colony would perish in its first infancy, like so many previous plantations of the New World.

Averse though his cheerful nature was to despondency, Thomas Warner could not hope that he and his companions would survive till the arrival of the expected ship from London. What if storms at sea had been even more unkind to the ship than storms at land had been to them? Even in a tropical climate corn does not grow and ripen in a few weeks; and the question that troubled the adventurers was how they should live for a few days.

Whilst calmly preparing himself for the worst, Warner exerted himself to mitigate the calamity which had befallen his expedition; and by the end of the following February (1624) he had another crop of tobacco ready for shipment. A few days later Captain John Jeaffreson brought his good ship the 'Hopewell' alongside the shore of St. Christopher's Island; and in a trice he had thrown his arms round his friend's neck.

Historian after historian has asserted that the 'Hopewell' was fitted out at the charges of James Hay, Earl of Carlisle. But the evidence to support this statement is still to be discovered. There is no proof that the brilliant and versatile nobleman had ever condescended to trouble himself about Transatlantic adventure and adventurers, when the 'Hopewell' dropt down the Thames. The first patent that ever passed the Great Seal of England in a matter relating to any plantation on the West Indian islands—a patent bearing date the 13th of September, 1625—makes particular mention of Thomas Warner's discovery of " fower several Islands in mayne ocean toward the Continent of America, the one called the Island of St. Christopher's, *alias* Merwars Hope ; one other, the Isle of Mevis; one other, the Isle of Barbados; and one other, the Isle of Monserate, which said Islandes" are declared in the same document to be "possessed and inhabited only by savage and heathen people," and never up to the time of their discovery by the same Thomas Warner to have been "in the possession or under the government of any Christian Prince, State, or Potentate." The same writing makes special mention of Ralphe Merifield's services in setting forth and supplying King Charles the First's "well-beloved subject, Thomas Warner, gentleman," and in having "alsoe byn the means of transportinge our well-beloved John Jeaffreson, gentleman;" but the patent makes no mention whatever of James Hay, Earl of Carlisle, who, like the patron mentioned in Samuel Johnson's letter to Lord Chesterfield, appears to have come to the help of the adventurers when they had no longer any urgent need of his assistance, and when he imagined it would be to his certain advantage to associate himself with them.

It is not credible that if the Earl had fitted out the 'Hopewell,' the above-quoted patent of the commission to Thomas Warner,

John Jeaffreson, and Ralphe Merifield would have been silent on the matter, at a time when (if the historians may be trusted) the nobleman was already soliciting his Sovereign for a grant in perpetuity of all the Caribeean Islands, including Barbadoes.

Before the end of the first year of Charles the First's reign, the Earl did unquestionably obtain this preposterous grant; but instead of getting it for the advantage of the adventurers, he obtained it to the manifest injury of Thomas Warner and John Jeaffreson, who were thereby deprived of all the power and privileges accorded to them by the patent, which had granted, only *during pleasure*, the lieutenancy of the already named four islands to Thomas Warner, and contained the following passage, conferring, in case of Warner's death, the same lieutenancy on John Jeaffreson :—" And our farther will and pleasure is, that in case the said Thomas Warner be at this present dead, or hereafter shall die, our Lieutenant as aforesaid, then and in that case, we doe hereby authorize and appoint the said John Jeaffreson, if he be then livinge, in his room and place. And we doe hereby give and grant unto him the like power, authority and preheminence during our pleasure as is before by these presents lymitted, meant or mentioned to the said Thomas Warner, and if in case the said John Jeaffreson be at this present dead, or hereafter shall die, our lieutenant as aforesaid, then our English subjects being or which shall be resident in the said islandes shall and may elect some other able and fitte person there resident to be our Lieutenant."

The fact seems to be that Lord Carlisle had no connection with West Indian adventure till full eighteen months after the 'Hopewell' left London.

When the historians patched up their untrue narrative, the copy of Charles the First's Commission to Thomas Warner and John Jeaffreson and Ralphe Merifield had not been calendared or discovered at the London Record Office. Nor had the original Commission, still in the hands of Sir Thomas Warner's descendants, been published in

"Antigua and the Antiguans" (1844.) Had Mr. Bryan Edwards, of Jamaica, seen the writings, which he might have inspected in Antigua, he would have made several alterations in his account of the colonization of the West Indies by the English.

It may not, however, be inferred that the Earl of Carlisle was wanting in consideration for the two joint-planters of the first English colony ever planted in the West Indies.

It is true that through his action they lost advantages that depended solely on a sovereign's "pleasure" and sense of justice. But the Earl did not omit to make them some compensation and atonement. Thomas Warner (or *Sir* Thomas Warner, as he became in 1629,) was appointed Deputy-Lieutenant of all the noble grantee's West Indian possessions; and John Jeaffreson, who had already appropriated, with Warner's sanction, a large breadth of ground in St. Christopher's Island, was endowed by the Earl's bounty with an additional thousand acres of land.

Having become a large landed proprietor in St. Christopher's Island, John Jeaffreson imported slaves and built a mansion that was long regarded as one of the grandest houses in the island. He also invited several of his Suffolk kindred and acquaintance to come out to him and participate in his prosperity. Amongst the first and the quickest to accept the invitation was the adventurer's brother, Captain Samuel Jeaffreson, who acquired the Red House Plantation, and died in the Red House on the 12th of December, 1649, when he was interred in his parish church, where his large tomb is preserved; Sir Thomas Warner having died in the same island on the 10th of March in the previous year, when he was buried in the Old Road Church at a spot covered by another rectangular tomb.

Captain Samuel Jeaffreson's only son settled in Antigua, where one of his descendants was a judge in the closing years of the last century. Another of the Captain's lineal descendants migrated to Virginia, where the name was changed to Jefferson.

On glancing at the terms of Charles the First's Commission to his beloved subjects, Thomas Warner, John Jeaffreson and Ralphe Merifield, the reader is surprised to see Barbadoes one of the four islands selected by the adventurers. Not only is Barbadoes much larger than the kind of island which the three partners deemed most eligible for their purpose, but its remoteness from the other three islands must have appeared a reason why it should not be associated with them in the Royal Charter. "Barbadoes" is unquestionably the name that appears in the original patent, and in the draft of the Commission preserved at the Record Office. But I have a strong suspicion that Warner made choice of Barbuda, a small island only fifty-three miles north of St. Christopher's Island, and so situated that no island lies between it and any of the other three islands named in the Charter. Whilst it is improbable that Thomas Warner desired to possess Barbadoes, it is quite possible and probable that the clerk who drew the patent, having only the vaguest and sketchiest notions about West Indian geography, wrote by mistake Barbadoes for Barbuda.

Anyhow, it is certain that the angry dispute between the Earl of Marlborough and the Earl of Carlisle, respecting their conflicting claims in the West Indies, had terminated in the arrangement which gave the sole property in Barbadoes to the latter Earl, before that island was systematically planted.

Nor does it appear that Warner took any prominent part in its plantation; though, as Lord Carlisle's representative, he doubtless had a voice and influence in its settlement.

Barbadoes is sometimes mentioned in histories and dictionaries as the oldest of the English settlements in the West Indies. For instance, Haydn puts its settlement in 1605. But the writers who give this date for the commencement of this colony are in error. Sir Olive Leigh's ship the 'Olive Blossom' no doubt touched at Barbadoes in

1605, on her way from London to Surinam; but all that her captain and crew did towards its plantation was to erect a cross (on the spot where James Town was subsequently built), inscribed with these words :—" James, King of England and This Island.". The first attempt to plant Barbadoes was made by Sir William Courteen's party of primitive planters, who, with Sir William Deane for their Governor, landed on the island at the end of 1624, nearly two years after Warner's commencement of work on St. Christopher's Island, and some nine months after the 'Hopewell' entered the Old Road.

Moreover, Courteen's enterprise was a failure. Having no heart to furnish them with needful supplies whilst his patron's dispute with the Earl of Carlisle was unsettled, the London merchant left the settlers to their own resources. The consequence was that, when the two peers had arranged their differences, the work of planting Barbadoes had to be recommenced.

West Indian history is singularly rich in false dates, baseless assumptions, and contradictory statements. On some points the confusion of authorities is unspeakably perplexing to the inquirer.

But there is no question that the English colony of St. Christopher's Island, begun in 1623, was the first English colony ever planted in the West Indies.

CHAPTER III.

THE PERILS OF PLANTING.

The Stream of Emigrants from England to the West Indies—Warner's Visits to England—His Character—Jealousy of France and Spain—Dangers surrounding the West Indian Planter—Spanish Insolence and Cruelty.—The Duke of Lerma and Don Lewis Firardo—Spanish Atrocities at Tortuga—The Massacre at Santa Cruz—Cromwell's Vengeance on Spain—Slaughter of the Caribees and their Expulsion from St. Christopher's Island—The Bucaneers—Their Character and Pursuits.

WITH the arrival of the 'Hopewell,' there was an end to Thomas Warner's fears that his plantation in St. Christopher's Island would perish in its infancy through want of succour from the mother-country. Nor had he for any long time much reason to apprehend that the fewness of his recruits would oblige him to confine his operations to a single island.

For some years no ship sailed from England to the West Indies without emigrants to St. Kitt's. Ship after ship, specially fitted and chartered to carry out new recruits to Warner's rapidly growing army of adventurers, left London, Ipswich, Harwich, Southwold, and Yarmouth. In 1625, and again in 1629, Warner crossed the Atlantic to exercise his personal influence in stimulating his friends to greater exertions in behalf of his enterprize. On the earlier of those visits to England, he made the personal acquaintance of the Earl of Carlisle, who could not fail to see that his lieutenant in the West Indies was a man of good breeding, uncommon tact, and inexhaustible energy. During the later visit he received the distinction of knighthood from Charles the First, at Hampton Court Palace, on the 21st of September, 1629. This compliment was doubtless serviceable in commending Warner's projects to the public; and though his influence on West Indian colonization has been greatly exaggerated, it cannot be questioned that the Earl of Carlisle's patronage of the new plantations was serviceable to their interests. But Sir Thomas Warner owed his success to his own remarkable powers rather than to his great friends. From the scanty particulars that have come to us respecting his character and career, it is obvious that nature designed him to be a leader of men, and endowed him in a singular degree with the power of winning the affectionate devotion of comrades. It was to his honour that, although he had sprung from no powerful or aristocratic family, his influence was nowhere greater than in the county and immediate district of his birth and boyhood.

Suffolk continued to send him a large proportion of his new settlers.

The number of those adventurers was so great that, having fairly planted the English district of St. Christopher's Island, he began to settle Nevis in 1628 (the year in which Massachusetts was first planted), and founded colonies in Antigua and Mountserrat in 1632, three years before the beginning of the first settlement in Connecticut. At the time of Sir Thomas Warner's death, the English population of St. Christopher's Island was computed at twelve or thirteen thousand; but this computation must have been excessive. Anyhow, the astounding success of Sir Thomas Warner's operations was the cause of fierce and vindictive jealousy to France and Spain. It was also the cause of a not unamiable mortification to the English settlers on the American main-land, who saw themselves so greatly surpassed by their countrymen of the islands.

Whilst Sir Thomas Warner was planting St. Christopher's Island, Nevis, Antigua, and Mountserrat, it devolved on John Jeaffreson to push forward the works requisite for the development of his estate, and at the same time to organize the military force of the first-named island.

As Colonel of the Militia of St. Christoper's Island, he had to drill foot-soldiers, train a regiment of cavalry, and construct fortifications. He was at the same time

Colonel of Infantry, Colonel of Horse, Colonel of Engineers, and Minister of War.

The West Indian colonist of the seventeenth century was at all times a fighting farmer. Every settler in a rude country, with an aboriginal population of jealous and crafty savages, watching his labours and nursing schemes for his destruction, holds his life on insecure and perilous terms. But the condition of the St. Kitt's planter was especially precarious. It is no figure of speech to say that he went to his daily toil with his sword at his side and with pistols in his belt. At any moment he might be called upon to throw down the hoe and draw the flashing blade.

He had to defend himself against the Caribees, the Bucaneers, the Spaniards, the French, the Dutch, and the vindictive treachery of his negro slaves.

The Spaniard was the object of his strongest and most abhorrent dread. At the present time, when Spain has sunk to be a by-word for pitiful weakness, it is difficult to realize the arrogance of her temper when she was greatly powerful. It is easier to imagine her former cruelty; but the imagination cannot, without an effort, render justice to the terrifying and disgusting ferocity of her unsubdued spirit. Having discovered the New World, she declared that it belonged to her; and that she had a natural and sacred right to put to slavery, torture, or death any Europeans who presumed to visit its vast and sparsely inhabited territories without her permission.

When Sir Charles Cornwallis entreated the Duke of Lerma to call the Spanish Admiral, Don Lewis Firardo, to account for sending to the galleys a number of English sailors, whose only offence was their presumption in visiting the West Indies, the Spanish Minister replied with exquisite politeness and a satanic malignity, "Surely, Don Lewis Firardo shall be called to account for sending your countrymen to the galleys, when he ought to have hung them." In a letter to James the First, Sir Walter Raleigh describes how certain Spaniards of the New World seized twenty-six Englishmen, tied them back to back, and then cut their throats; this revolting outrage being rendered all the more sickening, because the murderers had for a month been displaying every sign of friendliness to their victims, who were unarmed at the moment of the bloody assault.

In the year 1637 an overpowering force of Spanish marauders pounced down on the little English colony planted on the island of Tortuga, and killed with sword or rope every man, woman and child in the settlement. They even hanged the wretches who, after the fight, surrendered themselves on a promise that their lives should be spared. England had then no king with the heart and nerve to punish this monstrous crime. But when the Spaniards in 1650 repeated at Santa Cruz the carnage of Tortuga, and put the whole English colony to death, England was governed by Cromwell who, moving deliberately and resolutely, took possession of Jamaica, and inflicted on Spain such humiliation as she had not endured at English hands since the days of the Armada. The Protector's chastisement was signal; and so long as he lived, our West Indian planters were light of heart, though a Spanish fleet was visible from their tobacco fields.

But when Oliver had breathed his last breath, their old dread of the Spaniard revived, together with the reasons for it. Attacking the English colony on Providence Island (Bahamas) with an overwhelming force in 1680, the Spaniards put the inferior settlers to the sword, and seizing Governor Clarke roasted him to death on a spit. Similar atrocities were perpetrated by the Spaniards in the earlier decades of the eighteenth century. After boarding an English vessel in West Indian waters (*temp.* Geo. I.) and searching for contraband goods, a Spanish commander put the captain to the torture, and finished by cutting off his ear, which he bade him take home and show to the King of England. Captain Jenkins did better. Preserving his ear in spirits, he carried it back to England, and exhibited it to the House of Commons, together with his prayer for vengeance. "What thoughts, Captain," inquired a Member of the House, "passed through your mind, when you were in such a ruffian's power?"

"Sir," Captain Jenkins answered loftily, "I recommended my soul to God and my cause to my country."

Short work was made with the Caribees on St. Christopher's Island. Having learnt, or imagined themselves to have learnt, that the natives had prepared a scheme for their destruction and were on the point of putting it into effect, the European settlers took stern and perhaps needless measures for their self-preservation. Falling on the Caribees by night, they slew one hundred and twenty of their stoutest men; and having selected a few of their comeliest women for domestic service, they ordered the remainder of the aboriginal population to quit the island. This painful affair took place in 1625 or 1626.

After a short interval of time, which they spent in mustering forces from different islands, the banished Caribees reappeared in

St. Christopher's Island in the belief that they and their allies could conquer their enemy in fair battle. They estimated their power too highly. A sharp conflict ensued, and when it was over the field of battle was a hideous spectacle. The Europeans had lost one hundred soldiers; the miserable Caribees had lost thousands. Henceforth the ancient possessors of the soil left the intruders in undisturbed possession of the island.

On the authority of Du Tertre, whose book is curiously rich in blunders of every kind, English writers have followed one another in asserting that the Caribees of St. Christopher's Island were slaughtered treacherously and in cold blood. The statement is a calumny on civilization. The majority of the poor wretches were killed in open and hot fighting, that was greatly destructive to the conquerors. As for the night attack, it was a military surprise, not an affair of treachery. Nor was it done in cold blood. If the Europeans were misinformed as to the Caribeean policy, they at least made the attack in a genuine belief that it was necessary for their safety. They may have acted from panic. But however lamentable, acts done in hot and maddening panic should not be denounced as acts of frigid cruelty. On the other hand, it is certain that the Caribees were not the mild and placable creatures romance has depicted them, and that they repaid with execrable ingratitude and malice the tenderness exhibited to them by European settlers on other islands.

Under ordinary circumstances, the West Indian planter had little to fear from the bucaneers, so long as he remained on his island. It was not often that those maritime marauders landed on a feeble settlement, only to carry off the cattle and stores of a few planters. That they were capable of such exploits is proved by the repulsive annals of West Indian piracy. At the instigation of revenge, or from an unprovoked thirst for blood, they would sometimes seize a town, and after sacking it put the inhabitants to the sword. But outrages of this kind were unusual with them.

Their proper function was to lie in wait

for richly laden carracks and galleons, and seizing the happy moment, to run in upon them, grapple with them, board them, murder their seamen and passengers, and take possession of their treasure, their bars of precious metal, and their cargoes of tobacco, sugar, indigo, and spices. If the captured ship were worth the trouble, they towed it to one of their nearest havens. If it were cranky or seriously injured, they scuttled it and left it to sink. Such was the regular business of those strange highwaymen of the deep, who emulated the worst qualities of Elizabeth's maritime adventurers, and for several generations were a society that, living outside the bounds of lawful authority, and executing its own decrees for its own exigencies, offered not a few points of moral resemblance to the "outlaws" of Norman England.

Some of their leaders were ruffians of parts. A few of them preserved in their degradation some traces of the chivalric bearing and honest sentiment that had distinguished them in former time, when they were gentlemen.

It has been alleged in their behalf that they were not such villains as they have been painted. Sometimes it is suggested that they were not in all cases pirates. But the only ground for this last statement is that some of them were secretly attached to particular European Powers, and confined their predatory action as far as possible to times of war, when they could perpetrate acts of piracy under the authority of letters of marque. Yet even these more scrupulous freebooters of the sea, who held to their curiously selected points of honour, and shot every-one who accused them of being pirates, were capable of committing every kind of ocean robbery when they were goaded by want. On emergencies, they would also perpetrate pillage on land.

But though the West Indian planter of the seventeenth century troubled himself little about the bucaneers, so long as he remained at home, it was otherwise so soon as he embarked for a voyage to a neighbouring island. Once upon the ocean, he was a traveller on a road invested with highwaymen, and might at any moment have to fight for his life.

His insecurity, however, was due to European war more than to any other cause.

CHAPTER IV.

THE TWO NATIONS.

The Various Nationalities of the European Settlements in the West Indies—Incessant Conflicts of the Plantations—Their Participation in the Civil Commotions of the European States—West Indian Planters punished for their Loyalty to Charles the First and Charles the Second—Punished in the next Generation for adhering to William the Third—Origin of the French Colony on St. Christopher's Island—Sir Thomas Warner's Reasons for allowing the French to settle there—Mutual Jealousies and Animosities of the two Settlements—Successive Wars between the French and English on St. Christopher's Island.

EVERY nation of Western Europe had its settlements in the West Indies. There were Dutch and French, Spanish and Portuguese settlements; and no considerations could induce these settlements to discard their national prejudices, and disconnect themselves from the squabbles of the Old World. Whenever war broke out in Western Europe, they flew at one another with murderous zeal. At the same time, every European monarch with fleets at sea was on the alert to seize the Transatlantic possessions of any Power with whom he was at war on a purely European question.

Nor did their remoteness from Europe exempt the colonists from the inconveniences and penalties of participation in the civil commotions of their respective States in the Old World. Having taken Charles the First's part against the Parliament, and having on his death declared their allegiance to Charles the Second, the English planters of St. Christopher's Island were reduced to obedience by the forces which Cromwell sent out, under the command of Admiral Penn, for the conquest of Hispaniolas. After suffering in this manner for their fidelity to the House of Stuart under the Commonwealth, they were punished for their support of William of Orange some thirty-five years later; when they were driven from their possessions by the French West Indians who, following the example of their Sovereign in Europe, took James the Second under their patronage.

Surrounded by dangers in any of the plantations, the English planter was especially liable to military surprises in St. Christopher's Island, where a French colony had grown up side by side with Warner's settlement.

It has been often objected against Sir Thomas Warner that he showed himself wanting in sagacity and spirit in allowing some thirty Frenchmen to settle in the island nearly three years after he had occupied it for the King of England, and when he could easily have driven them from the coast. And it cannot be denied that the criticism is countenanced by events. But though he erred, Warner was not without excuses for his error.

His position was just then by no means so secure as his censors imagine. He had already discovered signs of unfriendliness in the Caribees, and he suspected them of nursing a project for the massacre of himself and his people. He had, moreover, become fully alive to the spirit and purpose of Spanish policy in the islands. At any moment, he and his people might have to fight the Caribees to the death. At any moment he and his people might be over-matched by a Spanish force. It was neither impossible nor improbable that they would be confronted by the two dangers at the same time, and that the crafty and cruel Spaniard would ally himself with the deceitful Caribee to check English progress in the New World.

Troubled by these apprehensions, Thomas Warner had no desire to strengthen the forces that aimed at his destruction. Nor was he in a mood to repel any adventurers who might strengthen his hands against the Indian and the Spaniard. When, therefore, D'Esnambuc and his thirty followers landed from their shattered ship on the coast of St. Kitt's, the English chieftain was much more disposed to welcome them as friends than to reject them as enemies. He had good reason to do so. The Frenchmen overflowed with hostility against the Spaniards, and the sincerity of their hatred was beyond question. D'Esnambuc, the captain of a French privateer, had barely escaped destruction by a Spanish galleon, which he had encountered in the open seas; and the circumstances of his conflict with the ship of superior strength had taught him that the Spaniards recognised no distinctions between European interlopers, but were bent on exterminating them one and all, without regard to their nationality.

It was under these circumstances that Thomas Warner, instead of attacking the beaten Frenchmen and driving them into the sea, made liberal terms with them. It was for the moment felt on both sides that, though they might be natural enemies in Europe, other conditions required them to be staunch and cordial friends in the West Indies. What were the discords of the Old to adventurers in the New World? The subjects of Charles and Louis might be bounden as much as heretofore to fight amongst themselves in Europe; but in the Transatlantic Islands they must join hands, and offer a bold and united front to the Spaniards. Warner at first seemed all the more justified in taking the conciliatory course, because D'Esnambuc enjoyed the patronage of the great Cardinal Duc de Richelieu.

Hence it came to pass that a colony of French adventurers was planted on the same island as the colony of English adventurers; and whilst the latter was increased by the strong and steady influx of recruits from Great Britain, the former was strengthened by the continual arrival of emigrants from France.

For the prevention of disputes between the two societies of settlers, the island was divided between them on May 3, 1637, by the Treaty of Partition, to which the writer of the ensuing letters makes reference. This same agreement comprised articles for perpetual amity and a league offensive and defensive, against all enemies whatsoever, between the two contracting parties; articles that reappeared in the draft for the more ambitious Treaty of Neutrality which the same writer, without entertaining any sanguine hopes of good results from the scheme, recommended forty years later to settlers of *all* the English and French colonies of the islands and the North American mainland.

Save that they had common roads, *i.e.*, an equal right to certain of the main thoroughfares through the island, and shared one or two other privileges, the English colony and the French colony were distinct communities. In matters of legislation and jurisdiction, they could not have been more distinct and independent, had they been separated by twenty miles of sea. Each had its own Governor, parliament, and army. Each had its own laws; and in some particulars the laws of the one settlement differed greatly from the laws of the other. Their good-will did not survive the urgent necessity for co-operation. The primitive settlers of the French party were no sooner confident of their ability to stand alone than they began to murmur against the encroachments and inordinate pretensions of the English. On the other side, our countrymen reflected severely on the ingratitude of the French people whom they had befriended in their adversity; and having more reason to fear

D'Esnambuc's malice than to value his friendship, they bitterly repented their former generosity to him and his associates. In fact the allied colonies were two distinct and dangerously near nations; and the proximity was fruitful of mutual distrust, jealousy, and resentment. The ensuing letters call attention to the selfish restrictions by which the French strove to limit the trade and lessen the prosperity of the English, and to the insolent demeanour of the former to the latter. Of course, the French told similar stories of English cupidity and arrogance.

Nor did this rancorous rivalry vent itself only in defiant speeches and vexatious enactments. It again and again broke out in war of the bitterest and most vindictive kind. For years before their first open combat, the two colonies had lived in a state of mutual animosity that was likely at any moment to become war; and in the forty-eight years which intervened between the Anglo-Dutch war of 1665 and the year 1713, when the Treaty of Utrecht secured the whole of the island to Great-Britain, they fought each other repeatedly, and never desisted from the miserable struggle without a secret resolve to return to it at the earliest opportunity.

During the above named Anglo-Dutch war, the French colony, with the aid of the Dutch in the West Indies, succeeded in driving the English planters from St. Christopher's Island; and it was not till the Peace of Breda that the last named colonists recovered the estates from which they had been expelled. In 1689 the French again made themselves sole masters of St. Christopher's Island; but on this occasion they had enjoyed their conquest for only eight months, when the tables were turned upon them by General Codrington, who gained a signal victory over their troops, and transported eighteen hundred of their people to Martinico and Hispaniola. From the clause in the Treaty of Ryswick (1697), which stipulated for reparation to the victims of General Codrington's severity, the French gained little advantage; but they had the satisfaction in 1705 of seeing the estates of the English planters of St. Christopher's Island again laid waste by French soldiers.

CHAPTER V.

A FORTUNATE ADVENTURER.

The Colonel's Retirement from St. Christopher's Island—His Services to the English Colony there—Conquest of the Island by Don Frederick of Toledo—The Colonel's Marriage—He commands a Ship in the Anglo-Dutch Naval Battle of 1653—His Wealth—His Death and Disposal of his Estates—The Letter-Writer's Education.

HAVING acquired his estate in St. Christopher's Island, built his house upon it, and settled the plantation in the rude and imperfect way in which such properties were settled in the seventeenth century, Colonel John Jeaffreson returned to Europe; leaving his West Indian land to the management of his brother Samuel, and his offices in the colony to younger aspirants for civil and military employment.

He had saved the colony from extinction in its second year, and he had helped Warner to carry it through its earlier trials. If there was aught blameworthy in the nocturnal attack on the Caribees, no small proportion of the blame must be awarded to him as a principal commander in the affair. The same may be said of the part taken by the English in the subsequent battle that resulted in the final expulsion of the Aborigines from the island. He was also in command of his Militia, when the arrival of Don Frederick de Toledo at St. Christopher's Island (1630), with twenty-four ships of force and fifteen frigates, afforded the colonists no single chance of success in resisting the overwhelming armament.

The conduct of the French on this occasion was not of a kind to make the English congratulate themselves on the pluck and bottom of their allies. After a feeble show of military purpose, the French abandoned their two forts, Basseterre and Capesterre, and taking to their boats, escaped to Antigua, leaving the English in the lurch. What followed is uncertain. The English are said to have retreated to the mountains, whence they sent deputies to treat for a surrender to the Spanish Admiral, who replied with an order for their immediate and unconditional submission. Thus far the usual story is probable. But one can scarcely believe the remainder of the narrative, which represents Don Frederick de Toledo as sending six hundred of the English colonists to work in the Spanish mines, and compelling the rest of them to quit the island instantly in some English ships which he had seized at Nevis. The order to leave the island was given, and it was doubtless obeyed by those of the settlers who came within the Don's reach. But they complied, only to return immediately on the departure of the Spanish fleet. The Spanish Admiral would, of course, carry off as slaves such of the able-bodied males as fell into his hands; but that he deported so many as six hundred stout Englishmen is improbable.

Certainly the chief persons of the colony were not captured. Having retired to the mountains, they may be presumed to have remained there with their people; till the insolent Spaniard, who was sorely pressed for time and anxious to accomplish the more arduous part of his mission to the Indies, could wait no longer for their submission. Anyhow, the Admiral had the satisfaction of laying waste the deserted plantations and homesteads, and maintained the prestige of his nation by perpetrating many acts of whimsical cruelty. Had not the Don outraged humanity, Charles the First would not have gained the superb reparation of the already mentioned treaty of peace and amity, which Spain treated as waste paper, even before the ink of its signatures was dry.

It was after his return from the West Indies that Colonel John Jeaffreson married Mary Parkyns; but in taking a wife, he had no intention to forego the pleasant excitements and profits of activity. In the famous naval battle between the English and Dutch, he commanded a ship of one hundred and forty men and thirty-six guns, under "the Rt. Hon. Col. Richard Deane, and Col. George Monk, esquires, Generals and Admirals;" his little boy (christened Christopher after St. Christopher's Island), the future letter-writer and agent in London for the Captain-General of Leeward Islands, being then just upon three years old.

The remaining years of his life were passed in London or East Anglia, and were occupied chiefly in buying land and managing his private affairs. How he came to be sufficiently rich to buy so much real property without exhausting his personal estate is uncertain. As the younger son of a small land-owner, he can have inherited no large property. Though she was of a gentle and brilliant family, Mistress Mary Parkyns, one of a younger son's numerous progeny, brought him no considerable fortune. Adventure in the West Indies had given him much land there; but, as the reader will see from the subsequent letters, the imperfectly settled West Indian estates of the seventeenth century did not enrich their owners rapidly. How then did this man of a roving career grow rich? Prize-money coming to him during the Anglo-Dutch war doubtless contributed to his prosperity. The capture of Spanish galleons may have done more for his affluence.

Anyhow, he bought considerable real estates, to which attention must be called, so that readers may see what was the letter-writer's social position.

In 1656 he bought the manorial property and farms pertaining to Dullingham House, hard by Newmarket in Cambridgeshire, from a branch of the historic family of Wingfield; and about the same time he bought from Sir Richard Wingfield the manor of Easton in the county of Suffolk. Towards the close of his career he acquired land in Felixtow and Trimley, Co. Suffolk, and the important estate of Roushall in the parish of Clopton, in the same county, as well as houses and lands in Woodbridge and Wickham Market. His will (proved at Doctors' Commons in the year 1660), shows that he had also sums of money (that were large in Stuart England, though they seem insignificant at the present date), put out on loan at interest. One of these sums (£4,000, lent to Colonel Morton, of St. Christopher's Island), resulted in the cause of "Jeaffreson, executor of Jeaffreson, against Morton and Dawson and others, Tertenants of Yarway," reported in "Saunders's Reports."

With the exception of Roushall, bequeathed to a nephew who was his executor and the guardian of the lad's property, Colonel John Jeaffreson left all his real estate in England and the West Indies to his only son, who was just ten years old at the date of his father's death. To the boy also was bequeathed all the large personal estate, with the exception of legacies which the Colonel left to his several nephews and nieces, and a sum of £2,000, which he set apart as a sufficient portion for his only daughter, often mentioned in the Letter Book.

Dying in 1660, Colonel John Jeaffreson survived Mary Parkyns by several years; and after the death of his children's mother, he married a second wife, who closed her widowhood with the second marriage, which caused her step-son, the letter-writer, to be a brother by affinity to her step-sons, James and Constantine Phipps.

For the education of his son Christopher, the Colonel made in his will a provision that is not more characteristic of the man than of the times in which he lived. Leaving the child's earlier education to the discretion and love of the cousin (who was appointed the child's guardian and the executor of the will), the Colonel directed that the young man should at the age of seventeen years be apprenticed "to a trade or calling fitting for him, under a man of good condition and conversation, till he be of the age of two-and-twenty, *to the end that he may not have the disposal of his person.*"

This direction was carried out in no illiberal spirit. Having received his earlier training at a school, where he had school-fellows who were his friends in subsequent years, the young man was apprenticed to " a man of good condition and conversation ;" but the apprenticeship did not preclude him from " spending two yeares of his nonage in France," where he passed his time in "seeing the most remarqueable things of that kingdome, as well as in learning the language." At the same time he acquired a knowledge of the principles and practice of business, that enabled him throughout life to be the conductor of his own affairs, and also qualified him to manage the affairs of others. And whilst he underwent this training his estate was so carefully nursed that, on the completion of his twenty-second year, he had the revenue of an affluent country gentleman, apart from the rents of his West Indian property, which was less productive of immediate benefit than abounding in promise of future enrichment.

CHAPTER VI.

FROM LONDON TO THE LEEWARD ISLANDS.

The Letter-Writer's Early Marriage—Death of his Bride—He determines to make the Voyage to St. Christopher's Island—Reasons for this Determination—His Departure from Billingsgate—Incidents of the Voyage—His Sojourn at Madeira—His Stay at Mountserrat—His Shorter Stay at Nevis—His Arrival at St. Christopher's Island.

ON coming into his property, the young man married a daughter of the Colonel George Gamiell, to whom he wrote a considerable proportion of the letters copied into the Letter Book, during his residence in St. Christopher's Island.

Had this marriage fulfilled all his anticipations of happiness from it, the course of Christopher Jeaffreson's life would perhaps have been different. Content with the pleasures of his home, he would have remained with her in Cambridgeshire, in his old manor-house hard by Newmarket Heath, whither the King and Court came so often for horse-racing and other rural sports. A yearly trip to London would have been his best opportunity for seeing the world; an excursion to his tenants on the Suffolk seaboard would have taken him for ten days every autumn from the circle of his Newmarket friends; and a triennial journey to his mother's family in Nottinghamshire would have satisfied his appetite for travel in distant parts. Had he ever declared his curiosity and desire to visit his plantations in St. Christopher's Island, a merry voice would have condemned the project as a foolish fancy; and an anxious, pleading smile would have convinced him that he had better remain at home.

But the young wife dying soon after the marriage, a childless widower was glad to escape from his Cambridgeshire manor-house and turn his back on every spot that reminded him of her.

For a few months he stayed with his only sister, Madam Brett, of Channell Row, Westminster, " near the Mum-House," diverting himself with the whims and humours of Charles the Second's London; when having recovered something of his former cheerfulness of mind and manner, he recurred to an old purpose of his boyhood, and bethinking himself of his West Indian estate, determined to visit it.

It had been the dream of his youth to make this voyage. From his childhood, the light and glamour of romance had clothed his conception of that part of the world, where his father had fought the Indian and the Spaniard, and raised himself from poverty to affluence. Some of his near kindred lay buried in those islands, of which he had heard so much from his Suffolk cousins, who were never crossed in sport or love but they thought of seeking consolation on a tobacco-farm in the tropics. Since his nonage he had more than once blushed to think how easily and indolently he was living at an age, when his father was roughing it at sea and meeting danger at every turn.

And now there were reasons why he ought to go to St. Christopher's Island.

For some years his whole interest in that island had been farmed at a fixed rent by Mr. Worley, a member of the St. Christopher's Assembly, and a prominent person in the English colony; and of late Mr. Worley had been suspiciously slow in paying his rent. Moreover, it was reported to the young proprietor that his property was neglected by Mr. Worley; that settlers were unlawfully squatting on his land, and might acquire title to portions of it if they were not disturbed or brought to account; and that the time had arrived for adopting a new agriculture and making the disorderly and dilapidated plantation a great property.

One of the persons with whom the young man discussed his project for visiting the West Indies, was his first-cousin, William Poyntz, upholsterer, at the sign of the "Goat," in Cornhill, near the Royal Exchange, London. Like his cousin Christopher, William Poyntz was a grandson of Aden Parkyns, of Nottingham. He had also a West Indian pedigree through General Poyntz, whom, in the time of the Commonwealth, Charles the Second had appointed to be Governor of the English colony of St. Christopher's Island. Mr. Poyntz was urgent with Christopher to make the voyage; and at his suggestion it was arranged that the voyager should take out goods to sell on his own account, and other goods to sell on the account of William Poyntz of Cornhill.

There was a large gathering of gentlemen and ladies on the morning of the 16th of February, 1675-6, at Billingsgate, to drink the parting glass and wish a hearty farewell to the young man, who, on escaping from the throng of his well-wishers, dropt down the river in a rowing boat, in company with his sister, her husband Charles Brett (a gentleman-pensioner in ordinary at Whitehall), and two or three familiar friends. At Gravesend he went on board the 'Jacob and Mary,' (150 tons and sixteen guns; Master, Andrew Vandevell), at seven o'clock P.M., and in another hour was under sail for the Indies. Together with a heavy freight of merchandize, to be bartered in the plantations for tobacco, sugar, and indigo, the adventurer took out with him four English servants.

It was a fortunate but dilatory and devious voyage. Six weeks after leaving the Thames, the voyager and his companions were only at the beginning of a pleasant sojourn in Madeira, and it was the 9th of May before the 'Jacob and Mary' touched at Mountserrat. As the guest of the English Consul in Madeira, the adventurer saw Funchial under favourable circumstances; visiting its churches and religious houses, drinking its finest wine at hospitable tables, studying the curious manners of the Portuguese populace, and hearing marvellous discourse of the Enchanted Island, which so many mariners had seen, though none had reached it. None but idle talkers could think this island the mere fancy of disordered imaginations, for was it not noted as a geographical certainty in the maps and charts of His Majesty's Admiralty?

Having run for a hard life from a Turkish pirate before they arrived at Madeira, the voyagers in the 'Jacob and Mary' encountered storms and some danger from a bad leak before they reached Mountserrat, where the principal passenger was carried off to Governor Carroll's house, and in a trice found himself on terms of friendship with some twenty or more well-educated gentlemen and ladies, whose names were doubtless familiar to him, though he now for the first time looked upon their faces. There were excursions to be made in the picturesque island, where to the stranger (who had never before visited the West Indian islands, and yet had from his infancy heard so much of their natural features) every object was at the same time novel and old, so strange and withal so familiar. There were also brave dinners of turtle, and lubricous fish, and curiously flavoured wild-fowl, taken in the island or imported from other parts of the Indies. To-day the banquet was at Government House; on the morrow Madam Reade, Colonel Reade's widow, gave the feast. Nor were Captain Hodges, Captain Bromley, and Mr. Liddall and their wives less bountiful of their good cheer, and kindly greetings to the young man whose father, something more than half-a-century since, had run the 'Hopewell' into St. Christopher's Island, and played a foremost part amongst the primitive planters of the British West Indies.

No doubt the company was wanting in variety. Precisely the same faces and costumes appeared day after day at the different tables. The party of yesterday was the gathering of to-day, and would be the assembly of to-morrow. In respect to apparel, nothing was deficient in the gentlewomen, who were as brightly and richly clad as any ladies of their degree in Lincoln's Inn Fields or Soho. No less may be said for the men, who wore as much point and gold lace as any gallants loitering in the Mall or ogling saucy damsels in Spring Gardens. But the talk of these gaudy gentlefolk turned rather too much on the ruling prices of sugar and indigo, the damage done by the last hurricane, and the ineradicable wickedness of negroes. The cookery, however, was good, and the Madeira (the only wine esteemed by the West Indian Planters) was superb.

Bidding his hospitable friends at Mountserrat adieu, young Christopher went on in the 'Jacob and Mary' to Nevis, where, in the absence of the Captain-General of the Leeward Islands (General Sir William Stapleton) he went to the house of Colonel Russell, the Captain-General's brother-in-law, and Governor (or, to speak exactly in the manner of the time, Deputy-Governor) of Nevis Island. If the guest on this occasion saw the colonel's youngest sister, Fanny, he was far from imagining in how short a time the eleven-years-old girl would win his heart and lure him into making her an offer of marriage.

Having moved all his freight and baggage from the ' Jacob and Mary' to a shallop, Christopher with his servants went on board the last named craft, and, after a three days' sojourn at Nevis, made the passage to St. Christopher's Island, where they arrived on the night of 24th May, 1676.

Christopher was then at the happiest of all ages for a man of sufficient education, easy means, and sound constitution. He was twenty-six years old.

It is pleasant to imagine the spirit which animated him on waking from his first night's rest on the island after which he had been named: the emotions which stirred his breast as he took his first walk on the dark grey loam, so light and porous that it needs no implements for its culture but the hoe and the rake: the gladness which thrilled him as he sauntered companionless through deliciously cool groves, whose foliage formed an impenetrable defence against the sun, whilst the day-breeze danced round the twigless and leafless stems of the palmettos and the ceibas: the proud self-consciousness with which he mounted horse for his first ride round his paternal acres in the New World.

CHAPTER VII.

IN WHICH THE LETTER-WRITER FIGURES AS STOREKEEPER, PLANTER, AND MEMBER OF PARLIAMENT.

Christopher's Store—The Poverty of his Island—Trade without Money—Current Value of Sugar and Indigo—Freights of Merchant-Adventurers from London to the West Indies—Goods sold at the Store—Dearth of Labour in the Colony—Wages of skilled and common Workmen—Emigrants reluctant to settle in the West Indian Islands—Honest but poor Mr. Worley—His neglect of the Letter-Writer's Property—Christopher resolves to turn Planter—His Difficulty in ascertaining the Boundaries and Titles of his Properties—He becomes a Member of the Colonial Assembly—The Arrogance of the French Colony—Mutual Animosities of the two Nations—The Battle between the French and Dutch at Tobago.

ON his arrival in St. Christopher's Island, Christopher lost no time in offering his freight of miscellaneous commodities to the colonists. Twelve days after his landing, he could write to his cousin, William Poyntz, that he had opened his store in a convenient place, and was doing business with planters and inferior whites.

Though he would not despond, the condition of the Island was not inspiriting to the merchant, unfamiliar with the tastes and usages of its inhabitants. From one point of view the islanders were wretchedly poor, though they were fairly housed, sufficiently clothed, and well fed. They had things in abundance, but no money. Trade, retail as well as wholesale, was for the most part done on long credits; and when a customer paid for goods delivered, he made payment in tobacco, indigo, or sugar. In fact, every transaction over the store-counter was an affair of barter. When a planter bought a piece of cloth, or his wife a silk dress newly imported from London, the article was paid for in kind. Servants took their wages in sugar. Estates were sold for sugar or tobacco. When Christopher bought a choice mare for his own riding, he agreed to pay so many thousand pounds of sugar for the animal. With the same product of the soil he cleared his account with the agent of the Royal African Company, who supplied him with slaves. In barter any commodity did service for money; but indigo and sugar were the recognized currency of the Island, and universal substitutes for gold and silver— the pound of indigo being rated as two shillings, whilst the pound of sugar had the value of three halfpence. " Nor have I received," Christopher wrote to his cousin William Poyntz on the fifth of June, 1676, " a pound of sugar nor of indigo (except of two or three persons), for all the sales which I have made, which have been pretty considerable."

The usual freight of a ship, leaving the Thames for the West Indian islands in the seventeenth century, consisted of such articles of food as cheese, butter, herrings, pilchards, and corn-beef; such household commodities as candles and soap; such articles of furniture as chairs, bedsteads, cheap carpets, common pottery, inferior table-glass, draperies for curtains and linen sheets; such things and materials of apparel as hats, (beaver and straw), boots, shoes, ready made coats and breeches, stockings, pieces of serge, baize and broadcloth, and articles of millinery; such miscellaneous commodities as tools and utensils of hardware, harness for horses, arms and gunpowder.

On touching at Madeira, the adventurer with such a freight trucked a considerable part of it for the wine of the island, and then went onward to Barbadoes, Nevis, or Jamaica. In return for his goods from London and his wine from Funchial, he took the tobacco, sugar and indigo of the West Indian planters.

The show of goods in Christopher's store accorded for the most part with the needs of the colonists. But both he and William Poyntz had over-rated the affluence of the plantations, and their demand for articles of elegance and luxury. The Cornhill upholsterer is cautioned not to send out any more bed-ticks, cloth-coloured serges, striped curtains, common carpets, buckrams, printed stuffs and cushions. "Too many of these things," the adventurer writes, "would soon cloy the country, because they are not but for the better sort. The most part here lay in hammakers, sit upon benches, cloath themselves in camies or some finer linen, and never cover the table but at meales." Christopher's Smyrna carpet and costliest cotton hangings would probably have remained unsold, had he not found a purchaser for them in Lady Stapleton, the wife of the Captain-General of the Leeward Islands :— the price of the Smyrna carpet being 1700 lbs. of sugar (about £5 5s. 0d. of money at its present value), whilst the four pieces of hangings were valued at 5000 lbs. of sugar.

But Christopher was quick to see that his father's colony suffered far more from want of labour than want of money. If barter was attended with serious inconveniences, it had also advantages which would be removed by an abundance of gold and silver. But the scarcity of workmen was an unqualified evil, from whatever point of view it was regarded.

The fertile and easily cultivated soil of the island would yield the finest indigo and the best sugar in prodigious quantities, if only workmen could be found to tickle it with the hoe, and turn its marvellous fruitfulness to good account. Our adventurer had not been a fortnight in the island before he wrote to London, imploring that workmen might be sent out to him. Of masons and carpenters he was in especial need; but he also required other skilled workmen and common field-labourers. The same cry is raised all through his letters; and to supply the one great want of the West Indian planters he by turns petitioned the English government for grants of convicts, and stirred the Royal African Company to send more negroes to the Leeward Islands.

At the present date, the terms offered to London craftsmen and English labourers of Charles the Second's time to induce them to emigrate to the West Indies, appear illiberal; even when full allowance is made for the great value of money, and the general indigence of the populace in Stuart

England. It was usual for an English workman, bent on seeking his fortune two hundred years since in the West Indies, to get an engagement before quitting his mother-country, and to bind himself to serve for four years the planter who paid the charges of his passage from the Old to the New World. During his four years of bond-service, the voluntary emigrant received board, lodging, and clothing from his employer, but no wages (either in "kind" or money) till his term was completed. On the expiration of the four years, the skilled artizan received 4000 lbs. of sugar, worth £25 sterling in Charles the Second's time, and about £125 at the present value of money; the ordinary labourer receiving sugar to the value only of £1 17s. 6d. sterling of Charles the Second's currency, or about £9 7s. 6d. of present money. But though these terms seem parsimonious; it is obvious from several passages of his letters that Christopher thought them ample and exceptionally good wages.

Anyhow, they failed to attract a sufficient number of honest emigrants. And in this fact is seen the chief and immediate cause of the decadence of the English colony of St. Christopher's Island since Sir Thomas Warner's death in 1648. The primitive planters had an abundance, indeed a superabundance of European recruits of the best quality; but the first rage for West Indian adventures having subsided, the supply of emigrants diminished. Moreover, the petty tradesmen and peasants of the old country received discouraging reports touching the insecurity of life in the islands, which were infested with pirates, destructive fevers, and bloody wars. The bucaneers and European privateers scared timid husbandmen from the islands, that had acquired an unenviable notoriety in Bristol and London from the execrable doings of the kidnappers. Whilst the islanders were compelled to get their supplies of labour from the African slave-ships and the English gaols, the current of free emigration went for New England, where life was supposed to be more orderly, decent, and devout.

Whilst minding the business of his store,

and accepting the hospitalities of the planters, Christopher was pressing Mr. Worley to pay arrears of rent, and making inquiries as to the tenant's ability to fulfil his obligations.

At Mountserrat, and again at Nevis, the young landlord had heard much that was false, and much that was true about his tenant. No one on those islands was ignorant of Mr. Worley, who had acquaintances everywhere, from Barbadoes to the North American mainland. As a member of the Assembly, and occupant of the best plantation of St. Christopher's Island, the loquacious, profuse, and pliant Mr. Worley had for some years been buying popularity at his landlord's expense; and by the time young Christopher came upon the scene, Mr. Worley possessed the good word, and bad opinion, of every-one who had taken advantage of his mental and moral weakness.

Sometimes Christopher heard him described tenderly as "poor Mr. Worley," and, at other times, heard him extolled as "honest Mr. Worley." Not a few of Mr. Worley's friends regarding him on both sides of his reputation, called him " poor but honest." A landlord likes to be told that his tenant is honest; but he is apt to question the statement when it is accompanied with the assurance that the honest man is nearly insolvent. Christopher knew enough of the West Indian world to suspect that the general compassion for Mr. Worley's poverty was attended with a secret sentiment that it was richly deserved. When he had been a few days in St. Christopher's Island, where the social regard for the defaulting tenant was enthusiastic, Christopher was not surprised to come on conclusive proof that Mr. Worley was a fool and a rogue —a bankrupt and a knave.

The several properties of the one straggling estate had been grossly neglected. Here they showed a few canes, and there a patch of indigo; but the grower of these scattered growths had neither the energy nor the capital to farm a tenth part of the land in his holding. His few negroes and cattle could not have worked a small plantation profitably. His embarrassments were overwhelming; and when he learnt that his young landlord was taking steps to put a distraint on the estate, honest Mr. Worley made his personal property over to a few selected creditors, and escaped to a part of the island where debtors enjoyed immunity from arrest.

It was clear to the proprietor that, if he meant to derive any considerable advantage from his West Indian plantations, he must stay in the island till he had thoroughly settled the property. He left England with the intention of spending from fifteen months to two years in the Indies. To settle the estate was a task that would require at least five years of his life. Should he make the sacrifice? Or should he leave the plantation to its fate, and return to the amusements of London and Newmarket? He was not long in coming to a conclusion. On the 22nd of June, 1676, when he had been just a month in the island, he wrote to his cousin, William Poyntz :—

"I have noe more to request of you at present, but that you would if possible procure me a carpenter and a mason. They would bee verry useful to mee, now that I am about to setle my plantation myselfe. For I intende to turne planter, and to set up a sugar worke, which will cost me some pence, but much lesse if I could have such servants."

At the same time he requested that his law-books—in particular, the folio called "Cooke upon Littleton," and a little law-book entitled "The Compleat Sollicitor,"—might be sent out to him; "for every one," he says, "is a lawyer in these partes."

Hitherto the St. Kitt's planters had not done much in sugar. But the opinion was gaining ground amongst the best farmers of the island that their soil was much better suited to sugar than tobacco; and that the planter, who aimed at making his fortune by a steady business rather than by speculative ventures, should prefer to expend his care on a comparatively sure crop like sugar, rather than on such a ticklish and capricious crop as indigo. Adopting these opinions, Christopher resolved to be the largest sugar grower, and have the best sugar-works in the island.

To ascertain the precise boundaries of his estate was impossible. But the young proprietor bestirred himself for the discovery of his titles and land-marks. For a time, he was troubled that he could find no deed demonstrating his father's title to the chief residence and property of his estate; but on reflection he accounted for the absence of a conveyance by the nature of the acquisition. There was the charter of Lord Carlisle's compensatory grant of a thousand acres. There was the indenture which proved that Serjeant Delve held his land under lease from Colonel John, and was therefore a tenant of the Colonel's heir. But, of course, there was no deed of conveyance for the main sweep of property, which the captain of the 'Hopewell' took from the Caribees to himself, before the great Earl had any interest in the West Indies, or King Charles the First had taken St. Christopher's Island under his gracious protection. Another territorial question to be answered, was to whom pertained the fee-simple of Garbrant's "large slip of land." There were manifest reasons for the opinion that the Dutchman, Garbrant, had with the aid and connivance of Delve fraudulently gained possession of an important piece of the Colonel's property. Then again, what of truth was there in the current story that Mr. Helote's plantation on the windward side of the island belonged to Colonel John's only son? For information on these and other like questions, Christopher wrote to his cousin John Jeaffreson of Suffolk, England—the cousin who had been his guardian and tutor—a long letter that affords some curious illustrations of the informal way in which land was acquired in the West Indies by the primitive planters.

Ejected from the plantations, which had suffered so much from his neglect, Mr. Worley dropt out of the Legislative Assembly through his loss of the material qualification of a member; the seat thus vacated in the Chamber being, of course, supplied by the letter-writer, who forthwith took an active part in the politics of the island.

When the Assembly withdrew its allowance from Lieutenant George, who had failed to show due zeal in discharging the functions of Political Agent (or Commissioner, as he would be termed now-a-days) in London for the English planters of St. Christopher's Island, Christopher insisted on the claims and qualifications of his father-in-law for the honourable and lucrative post.

Of course, the new Member of Assembly watched the mutual jealousies of "the two nations," as the *two* colonies of the island were usually designated by the planters, who compared them or regarded them together. He saw how the trade of each settlement was depressed and crippled by the protective policy of the other. It irritated him to observe the signs of French arrogance, and to know that the French was for the time by far the stronger of the two colonies. The military weakness and commercial difficulties of the English colony were all the more grievous to him because they were results of the war of 1666, which had been alike beneficial to the French and disastrous to the English planters. For the moment the two nations were exchanging professions of friendship; but the professions were hollow, and underneath the thin covering of simulated amity, the discords and animosities of the rival communities waxed fiercer. Whilst both sides talked in favour of the proposed Treaty of Neutrality, that would bind all the French and English settlements of the islands and of the main-land in a league of everlasting friendship, the English were thirsting to avenge the outrages of '66, and the French were resolving to affront the English as soon as their own little difficulty with the Dutch was disposed of.

Matters were in this state when the French and Dutch fell upon one another at Tobago, and gave the world a specimen of "the hottest service that many ages can tell of." For days and weeks before this smart affair, the waters about St. Christopher's Island had been alive with Dutch privateers, that crept close up to the island, stealing round its bold rocks, even as far larger vessels of the nineteenth century are wont to navigate the deep waters about the island, coming so near to shore that those on board can talk with those on land in their ordinary voices.

The planters were still in the first full enjoyment of the details of the great battle at Tobago, and Governor Matthews's little son (a lad of fourteen years, who had gone as a volunteer with Count D'Estrées against the Dutch) was tasting the first intoxicating draught of military glory; when Christopher's friends were sending out to him from England the goods and apparatus which he had ordered for his store and his sugar-works.

CHAPTER VIII.

UNDER ARMS.

Ensign Thorn of the St. Kitt's Militia—His Endowments and Chief Ambition—West Indian Stewards for Absentee Proprietors—A Short Life and a Merry One—West Indian Morality—Edward Thorn on his Good Behaviour —His Mission to London and his Victims there—A Man of Straw passing for a Man of Capital—An Alarm of War between England and France—War Panic in the Leeward Islands—In Garrison and on Guard—The French Fleet reinforced by Bucaneers—The Alarm at Nevis— Departure of the Fleet and Subsidence of the Panic— Hurtful Consequences of the Alarm—Bad News from England—The Store at Wingfield Manor.

THE time has now arrived to mention a person who plays a conspicuous part in the drama of the ensuing letters : Edward Thorn, supercargo and accountant, for some years known in the Leeward Islands as Ensign Thorn, of the St. Kitt's Militia.

A brisk, smart, personable young man, with ingratiating address, some knowledge of business, and a marvellous aptitude for taking to himself the property of those who trusted him, Edward Thorn would have been eminently successful in the West Indies, had prudence been added to his other qualifications. He lied exactly like truth; but sooner or later the falsehood, which no one suspected, was sure to be discovered by his own indiscretion. He robbed with matchless nerve and shamelessness, but he could not keep the wages of his dishonesty. A thief with one hand, he was a spendthrift with the other.

Nothing could be more creditable to him than the account he gave of himself, when he accosted Christopher one fine day at Nevis, and asked for employment. Christopher believed the fellow's story, liked his manners, appreciated his abilities, and engaged him to look after the store where Lady Stapleton bought her Smyrna carpet and hangings. Christopher was young enough to enjoy being a patron. Edward Thorn, who rightly valued his good fortune in getting so gracious an employer, determined to stick to him. Christopher made no secret of the fact that he was in St. Christopher's Island only for a time; that he should return to England when he had settled his plantation and started his sugar works. On his departure, having no wish for another tenant like honest Mr. Worley, he would need a steward. Edward Thorn resolved to be that steward.

Two centuries since, and long afterwards, to be the steward-in-charge of a large West Indian property was to have an enviable position. Master (*pro tem.*) of the great house, and lord of a hundred negroes or "bound whites," the steward did his will with the absentee's castle, cellar, stables, and slaves. There was no one to call him to account. However flagrant his misconduct, every report of it that reached his employer's ears was deemed the invention of slanderous malice, so long as the lieutenant sent to

London, or Bristol, the expected consignments of produce.

It might be supposed that self-interest would have restrained the steward from excesses that would, in the course of years, result in his downfall. In many cases prudence had that effect. But it often happened that a proprietor had no sooner set sail for England than his steward began to squander his substance in riotous living. The motto of such a steward was " A short life and a merry one." And it is significant of the morality of the West Indies in the times under consideration, that the profligate steward of an absentee master always enjoyed the countenance of his social superiors, and was voted a good fellow and a right honest fellow by the resident planters.

The West Indian proprietor, who made arrangements to live in England for several years, was a person to be plundered by the friends he left behind. His steward was encouraged to rob his master, on the understanding that the master's trusty friends shared the spoil. The right honest fellow was introduced to the best houses of the island; and he showed his sense of his protectors' goodness by " obliging" them with loans of his master's slaves and cattle, " accommodating" them with hogsheads of his master's best rum, and allowing them to deal with the absentee's estate as though it were the common property of all the good fellows of the island he had deserted. When the day of retribution came to the unjust steward, his patrons and confederates shielded him from the law's penalties, and softened his fall to the best of their ability.

Edward Thorn's highest ambition was to rule the plantation of an absentee proprietor; to put half-a-dozen field negroes into serge liveries; to give big dinner-parties to his employer's friends; to drink, swear, ride, gamble, wear a velvet coat, and go the pace with the maddest dare-devils of the English colony.

To achieve this lofty purpose, he determined to be Christopher's vigilant, obsequious, and indefatigable servant.

At first Edward Thorn's especial business was to keep the letter-writer's store in St. Christopher's Island, to wait on the customers, post up the accounts, transport the new goods from Nevis by shallop, deliver the articles bought by frequenters of the shop, take charge of the indigo and sugar deposited at the store in payment of bills, and superintend the shipment of such commodities for the London market. There was enough for the man to do, and Edward Thorn did it well. Having found him an indefatigable warehouseman, a trusty storekeeper, and a clever salesman, Christopher tried him as a buyer, and found him no less expert in choosing stocks than in vending them. In short, Edward Thorn proved himself a thoroughly capable agent.

Having tried him in smaller matters, Christopher dispatched his clever man to London, to buy goods for the store to the value of £200 sterling, which William Poyntz, of Cornhill, was duly instructed to give him. This commission was executed with judgment and dispatch; and Edward Thorn returned to the West Indies with a large cargo, made up of goods bought for Christopher, and of goods sent out by certain Londoners "for venture in the Indies." Mr. Penney, a London tailor, had trusted the adventurer with goods to the value of £35 or £40. Other London tradesmen had committed portions of their stock to his hands, on the understanding that he would sell the commodities to the best possible advantage, and send them the proceeds of the sales after deducting therefrom his proper commission.

Instead of telling Christopher how this additional cargo had been obtained, Edward Thorn asserted that he had bought it with money of his own. He had unexpectedly come in for gifts and a legacy that combined with his previous savings to make him a man of some capital. Though he had no wish to leave Christopher's service, still less to open a shop in rivalry with his store, Edward Thorn announced that he was rich enough to start as a merchant on his own account, and would some years hence be the largest store-keeper in the island.

Christopher was well pleased at his clerk's good fortune. It is natural for a capitalist to be readier to trust a man of money than a man of straw. Looking forward to the time of his return to England, Christopher thought he should do well to commit his West Indian interest to the stewardship of a young man who had property as well as parts.

Edward Thorn was still on the return voyage from London to St. Kitt's, when the English colonies of the West Indian islands received an alarm of war between England and France. The rumour caused the "two nations" on St. Christopher's Island to exchange looks and words of defiance, and to prepare for instant and deadly conflict as soon as the warlike news should be confirmed.

To render their unfinished fort capable of protecting the colonists and repelling the attack of a superior force, the planters and their negroes worked incessantly. All hands were withdrawn from field-labour, just at the season when the growing crops were in most urgent need of the weeder's care.

Whilst the slaves toiled with spade and mattock at earth-works, and the bond-whites conveyed stores of provisions and ponderous loads of costly furniture from the plantations to the fort, the freemen were under continual drill. From the middle of February, all through March, and far into April, this labour and excitement were maintained. Vigilant watch was kept on the movements of the French colony, whose Governor was in daily communication with the French Admiral D'Estrées, and the French Captain-General de Blanarque. Count D'Estrées, was understood to be waiting impatiently for Count de Blanarque's orders to open the war.

By the middle of April, the English colonists began to congratulate themselves on their security from immediate disaster. Their fort had been completed with earthwork and faggots; thirty pieces of cannon had been mounted on its walls; its stores of ammunition and victuals were sufficient; and it had a garrison of seven hundred white soldiers. Everyone was in good heart. Some of the more refined and gentle of the non-belligerents of course found their quarters inconveniently narrow; for the entire population of the settlement, white and negro, men, women, and children, were in the stronghold. On the 19th of April, the enemy's fleet in Basse Terre Road numbered thirty sail, for the French fleet under Count D'Estrées had been reinforced with a fleet of bucaneers. Every individual of the colony being required to assist the commonwealth to the *utmost* of his means, Christopher (as the largest and wealthiest landowner of the settlement) contributed largely to these defensive measures. His rank in the Militia was only that of a captain.

When it had spent some six or seven days in Basse Terre Road, keeping the occupants of the fort in lively excitement, this combined fleet of Frenchmen and bucaneers set sail, stood to windward, and bore down upon Nevis, where they occasioned a lively commotion. The latter island would not have been found unprepared had the naval armament tried to effect a landing. All the Militia of the island was under arms, a strong regiment of a thousand negroes had been drilled and provided with spears, every weak point of the coast exhibited an entrenched fort, and six hundred horses had been drawn from the plantations to transport the foot soldiers with speed to the stations where they were most needed.

But instead of assailing Nevis, the fleet sailed quickly past the island, tacked and stood southward.

Whether the force had been designed in the first instance for a demonstration against either of the settlements it had so greatly agitated, does not appear from the correspondence. Probably it would have swooped down on both of them had the preparations for resistance been less obvious and complete. Possibly the expedition had from the first an object remote from the two English colonies. Anyhow, so far as they were concerned, the whole affair was a mere alarm, entailing much expense of labour and injury to property, but having no bloody consequences. It was one of those "scares" that occurred at short intervals in the West Indies from the time of Charles the First to the time of George the Second.

The disappearance of the fleet having been followed by intelligence that England and France meant to keep the peace a little longer, the English colonists came out of their stronghold; the planters returning to their homesteads, and the negroes resuming their labour in the fields whose rising crops were choked with hurtful vegetation.

Christopher foresaw that in consequence of the alarm, he would be £200 sterling the poorer at the end of the year; and he had scarcely reconciled himself to this depressing certainty, when a letter from London informed him that he had lost the Chancery suit which was in progress, under Charles Brett's superintendence, when he left England. In reply, Christopher instructed his lawyers to renew the fight on any other ground that offered a chance of success.

For these misfortunes he was consoled by the success of his store. Every venture in that department of his speculations was successful. Barely four months had elapsed since Edward Thorn's return from London with a cargo of goods that cost £200, when Christopher wrote to London for more goods to the amount of £100. He was at the same time acting as a broker for William Poyntz and other adventurers in London, *i.e.*, selling their consignments of merchandise on commission. In connection with his activity in trade, it may be observed that, having closed the store in which he offered his first ventures for sale, he henceforth kept his shop at the great mansion house of his principal plantation.

The sentiment that the pursuit of trade clouded the honour and dignity of a gentleman was unknown to the West Indian planters of the seventeenth century. Every colonial governor was a dealer in something. The Captain-General did not disdain to turn an honest penny in retail trade.

103

CHAPTER IX.

CHRISTOPHER'S FOURTH YEAR IN THE WEST INDIES.

Depression of Agriculture—Dullness of Trade—Financial Trouble at Boston—The Proposal to appoint Colonel Gamiell to be London Agent for the Colony—The Treaty of Neutrality—The Letter-Writer's part in the Negotiations for the Treaty—Renewal of Alarms—The French Admiral D'Estrées courting the Bucaneers—French Insolence and Outrages—Failure of the Negotiations for the Treaty of Neutrality—Christopher's Store and his Venture in Horse-flesh—The Gallants of St. Kitt's.

THE fourth year of Christopher's residence in St. Christopher's Island was a year of trial and depression to the colonists. By causing the withdrawal of the workmen from the fields, when the canes and indigo had especial need of manual care, the alarm of war was a cause of serious loss to the planters. Christopher alone lost £200 sterling from this cause, a sum that may be computed at £1000 of money in these times.

Other circumstances increased the dullness of trade that necessarily resulted from the agricultural disaster. For commercial prosperity the islands were greatly dependent on merchants of New England, where various circumstances had caused financial trouble. The great fire had inflicted such injury on the Boston traders that they had little money or goods to speculate with. "But the New England men," Christopher wrote to William Poyntz, on 3 January, 1679-80, "who used to be the first at the markett, have probably beene kept back by the great unfortunate fyer which happened this summer in Boston, and haith much distracted the merchants, and put them out of their ways."

The year was more remarkable for political incidents than for commercial successes.

In the council and assembly of the English colony of St. Christopher's Island, there was much debate of the colony's need of a London agent, in the place of Lieutenant George, who had been dismissed for negligence. It was felt that an agent, without good social position, could not serve the plantation effectually. On the other hand the planters were so poor that they could not afford to give the new agent so large an allowance as they had rendered their previous representative. With much difficulty Christopher persuaded the council and assembly to offer the agency to his father-in-law, Colonel Gamiell, with a stipend of £100 per annum. But the intrigues of a party that desired the appointment of another person, resulted in the miscarriage of this arrangement at the last moment; and the colonists, to their serious inconvenience and prejudice, remained for some time longer without an advocate to plead for them before the Committee of Plantations and the Privy Council.

Another matter that occupied much of Christopher's time and care was the proposal for a Treaty of Neutrality, *i.e.* a league of perpetual amity and forbearance from war between the peoples of all the English and French settlements under the respective governments of Sir William Stapleton, the Captain-General of the Leeward Islands, and the Count De Blanarque, Lieutenant-General of the King of France by sea and land in America.

Though he had a strong opinion that, on any outbreak of war between Great Britain and France, no paper contract would avail to keep the peace between their West Indian dependencies, Christopher was inclined to think that the proposed treaty would have a desirable effect on the " two nations " of St. Christopher's Island, giving the one a reassuring sense of security from French outrages, and disposing the other to think that peace should not be broken, out of sheer insolence and wantonness.

As it was, the feeling between the two nations could not be worse. Admiral D'Estrées was still moving about with a strong fleet, and cultivating the good-will of the bucaneers. What was he after? At the same time the French colonists waxed strangely arrogant; breaking the ancient articles of concord, and questioning the right of the English to use the common paths. Every month had incidents that aggravated the mutual animosities and suspicions of the two peoples. Now an English soldier was found dead in one of the common paths, stabbed with forty-two stabs. Now the French Admiral ordered that English ships should not presume to enter the French waters, though from the days of Warner and D'Esnambuc the two nations had enjoyed unrestricted liberty in sailing round the island. A slave-ship, that had brought negroes from the Guinea coast, appearing off Nevis, the French fleet ran down upon her and seized her as a prize, alleging as a pretext for the act of piracy that she had entered French waters without permission. Of course, the object of the French was to get a cargo of slaves without payment. But fortunately the slaver had landed the great part of her black stock at Nevis before she was captured.

In the hope that it might improve a state of things which it could not render worse,

Christopher gave his cordial support to negotiations for the Treaty of Neutrality. Partly out of regard for his knowledge of the subject, and partly in consideration of his command of the French language, he was appointed to convey to the Count de Blanarque the amended articles of the league, which from some unaccountable caprice the French lieutenant-general refused to sign, though he had consented to them.

Whilst labouring to bring about the Treaty of Neutrality, Christopher was mindful of his private affairs. Notwithstanding the colony's poverty and the dullness of its trade, his store continued to flourish; and all the money that he made over the counter he threw into his plantation and sugar-works. In this year also he made a novel venture, sending Edward Thorn to New England to buy horses for sale in St. Christopher's Island. At the same time he had a care for his personal appearance.

"I praye you," he wrote, 7 January, 1679-80, to his sister, Madam Brett, of Channell Row, Westminster, near the Mum-

House, " send me an embroidered or fashionable waist-belt, and let everything be modish and creditable; for the better sort in these islands are great gallants, sometymes beyond their abilleties, or at least their qualleties."

CHAPTER X.

IN LOVE.

Christopher's serious Illness—Mortality of his Slaves—His Anxiety caused by Edward Thorn's Absence—The Agent's Return with a Cargo of Horses and Mares—The Letter-Writer recovers his Health and Spirits—Alarming Illness of Governor Matthews—The Princess of Nevis—Her Age and Fortune—Christopher is advised to make her an Offer of Marriage—His Friendly Relations with the Young Lady's Kindred—Value of Money in the days of the Stuarts—Christopher consents to accompany Colonel Matthews to England—The Colonel's Death—A Change of Plan.

THE earlier part of his fifth year in St. Christopher's Island was passed by Christopher in trouble and anxiety. Prostrated by a fever, which occasioned many deaths throughout the island, he rallied slowly; and whilst he was recovering his strength under circumstances that made him long to be again with his kindred and closest friends in England, he had the misfortune to lose several of his slaves from the malady which had almost put an end to his own life. "Of His mercy," the young man wrote to his cousin Poyntz, 3 August, 1680, "God hath restored us all to our healthes againe, excepting a few of my negro-slaves, some of whom death hath liberated from their bondage. These afflictions are bitter in the mouth, but sweet when digested. These bitter potions, which the Heavenly Physician seeth necessary for the soul, ought to be received with thanksgiving, not with murmurings."

But Christopher's resignation to the Divine will was not so complete as it ought to have been. He was not thankful for the loss of negroes whom he had bought at the high rates demanded by the Royal African Company for black cattle; and he murmured audibly at the unaccountable length of Edward Thorn's sojourn in New England. The agent having been entrusted with a large sum of money, his absence and silence occasioned his employer some painful suspicions and fears. If the affairs of his mission detained him, why did he not write by the ships that, in spite of tempests and violent gales at sea, continued to cross to and fro between the islands and the continent? Could it be that the young man, whom Christopher had taken to his familiar friendship and introduced to the best gentlemen of the Leeward Islands, would be found to have absconded with his employer's gold?

Fortunately Edward Thorn re-appeared in the middle of August with a story which, though it was no doubt for the most part untrue, made it appear that he had been a faithful emissary. A series of misadventures had occasioned him unlooked for difficulties and delays. He had written several times, but the captains he entrusted with his letters had been forced by foul weather to return to New England without visiting the Leeward Islands. As for his commissions, Ensign Thorn had executed them in every particular. Bills had been taken up, accounts paid, and orders given. Though he had narrowly escaped shipwreck on the return voyage, the agent had brought with him a goodly lot of horses and mares, that would not fail to get good prices, as soon as they had recovered from the effects of the voyage.

In the spring of 1681, Christopher was again in good spirits and perfect health. The trade of the islands was reviving, and his store, a lucrative concern even in periods of commercial stagnation, was yielding larger profits than ever. The plantations gave signs of an abundant year, and the sugar-works and distillery were fulfilling his most sanguine expectations.

Affairs had assumed this brighter aspect when Christopher was distracted by love and home-sickness. More than five years had passed since he parted with his acquaintances at Billingsgate, and dropt down the Thames in the company of the Bretts and Phippses. Naturally he pined to kiss his only sister again, and to crack his bottle and jokes with the comrades of his boyhood. At the same time Governor Matthews, whose health had been troubled by a painful disorder for many months, was bent on recruiting his constitution with a sea-trip and a stay in England. The Governor was urgent that his young friend should accompany him.

Whilst family affection and friendship for Colonel Matthews disposed him to start for England, another interest made him unwilling to leave "the islands" just then.

For some time he had been cherishing the tenderest and warmest of all sentiments for Mistress Frances Russell, of Nevis, who had been recommended to him as a good match by persons whose advice seemed to imply that, should he determine to assail her heart, he might entertain a confident hope of taking it. The daughter of Colonel Russell, the late governor of Nevis, and the sister of Sir James Russell, the present governor of the same island, Mistress Frances Russell was also the younger sister of Lady Stapleton, who, as the wife of the Captain-General, was the first lady of the Leeward Islands. At Nevis, which Sir William

Stapleton had made the seat of his government, Lady Stapleton was a queen and her sister a princess. The younger sister was also a princess of great beauty and a considerable fortune. On the completion of her sixteenth year, or on the day of her marriage, she would come into possession by her father's will of £1,500 and four negroes. At present she was still in her sixteenth year, an age at which young ladies were thought ripe for marriage in the West Indies, two hundred years since.

The young lady's nearest kindred wished to see her become Christopher's wife. Lady Stapleton had set her heart on the match. Sir James Russell was on the friendliest footing with Christopher, and could not fail to see that his sister would, from a prudential point of view, do well to marry a man who, besides being a large planter in the West Indies, was a squire with a good estate in England. Sir William Stapleton had formed a high opinion of the young man's political address and capacity.

Certain passages of Christopher's letters

may seem to indicate that his suit of Mistress Fanny's hand was made at the instigation of self-interest rather than of love. And it cannot be questioned that he was sensible of the social advantages of an alliance that would make him a member of the Captain-General's family circle. Nor was he indifferent to the lady's fortune, for £1,500 in hand was thought a good fortune for a gentle damsel in the seventeenth century. Men of wide acres had a keen appetite for ready money in the days of the Stuarts. Two thousand pounds in that period had the buying power of £10,000 in Victorian England; and in the general dearness of gold and the scarcity of girls with money, a gentle maiden with £2,000 in her own hand and disposal had the prestige and financial attractiveness of a modern damsel with £20,000 for her portion.

But though he wrote fully to his sister and Colonel Gamiell of the prudential considerations which disposed him to make Mistress Fanny an offer, he was as thoroughly in love with the Princess of Nevis as a young widower could well be.

In consideration of the young lady's age, which in England would have caused her still to rank with children, Christopher determined to accompany Colonel Matthews to England, and to postpone his formal and decisive declaration to Mistress Frances, till he should have returned from the mother-country to the West Indies.

Scarcely, however, had he made this resolution when the plan was disturbed by the Colonel's death.

The particular considerations, which had made him arrange to re-visit England in 1681 having been removed by this event, Christopher changed his purpose, and decided to spend the next twelve months in the West Indies.

CHAPTER XI.

CHRISTOPHER'S LAST YEAR IN THE COLONY.

New Clothes—Rejected Addresses—The Great Hurricane—The Second Tempest—The Letter-Writer's Resolution to "go home"—He appoints Edward Thorn to take charge of his Plantations—A Colonial Farewell—The Captain-General confers with him on Matters of Public Interest—Sir William Stapleton entrusts him with Commissions to be executed in London—Homeward Bound—Arrival in London.

ON 25 July, 1681, Christopher wrote to London, begging that the next ship bound from London for the Leeward Islands might bring out for his use and adornment a new hat, enough broad-cloth and bright lining for a fashionable coat, a lace cravat and cuffs, a handsome sword-belt, and a pair of silk stockings.

The careless reader of the letters will be likely to assume that these articles of costume were ordered for his wedding by a suitor too little heedful of the adage which declares there may be slips between the cup and the lip. But the substance and tone of the letter, dated 28 July, 1681, just three days after the date of the order, forbids any such assumption.

The fact is that Christopher had received his first "brisque denyall" from Mistress Frances some seven or eight weeks, and his final rejection several days before he sent to London for the fashionable sword-belt and new pair of silk stockings.

Mistress Frances knew her own mind; and child though she was, Christopher was not the first suitor for her hand. One of her other admirers had so much reason to deem himself the captain of her dreams, that he "tooke strange measures in his amours," and boasted of his conquest to several of his friends. She was also surrounded by certain makers of mischief, who out of malice to Christopher, or spite to her family, infused her with jealous suspicions of him, whilst extolling the merits of his rival. The consequence was the miscarriage of Christopher's suit.

Having received his first offer with a silence which, far from discouraging the lover incited him to renew his petition on the earliest opportunity, Mistress Frances replied to the second proposal with a precision and decisiveness remarkable for a person of her age. Six weeks after this repulse, the pertinacious suitor tried to reopen the negotiations with a letter, which was answered in a manner that determined him to dismiss all thought of acquiring the young lady, her gold, and her negroes.

Christopher had not spent many days in deploring this misadventure, before his thoughts were diverted from the humiliation by one of the most violent hurricanes that had visited St. Christopher's Island within the memory of man. Beginning about two a.m., on Saturday 27 August, 1681, and lasting for forty hours, this storm of wind and rain took the roof from his dwelling-house, threw down the massive walls of his two sugar-works, blew most of the negroes' huts clean away, and made deplorable havoc amongst the canes and other crops. After an interval of some five weeks, when exertions had restored some of the buildings destroyed by the gale, a second hurricane swept over the island, to the demoralization of the slaves and mean whites, who had no sooner begun to recover from one tempest than they were beaten down by another.

Though they may have come opportunely to save him from brooding over his sentimental trouble, these trials did not strengthen Christopher's disposition to prolong his stay in the West Indies. On the contrary, they quickened his longing to return to his native land where the atmosphere is at least exempt from the violent commotions, though it may lack the luxurious warmth of a tropical climate. Other reasons concurred to set his mind towards England. More than five years had passed since he left the old country; and whilst letters told him that some of his nearest kindred had suffered in health during his absence, other letters certified that his presence in England was required by his affairs in London and his estate in the Eastern Counties.

It surprised none of his friends in the West Indies, in the June of 1682, to hear that, having re-roofed the Wingfield Manor House, and re-built his sugar-works, and seen his plantations recover from the disastrous effects of the great hurricane, he had taken the chief-cabin on board the 'St. Nicholas,' and would sail for England in the middle of the next month. Nor did it surprise them to learn that he had appointed Ensign Edward Thorn to act as his agent and steward on the island during his absence, which would probably cover, and much more than cover the five years, during which the said ensign had by indenture bound himself to be the true and loyal servant of his employer and patron.

The news, however, made a stir; and during his sojourn in the West Indies, Christopher had made himself so popular with the gentry of his particular colony, that they assembled (women as well as men) from every part of the settlement to drink to his honour and prosperity in bumpers of choice Madeira, and to attend him from his house to the spot where he went on board. Some of the good people were so earnest in showing him respect that they refused to shake hands and part with him until they had seen him fairly on his ship.

A more gratifying expression of the esteem in which the leading colonists held him, was afforded by spontaneous action of the Captain-General of the Leeward Islands, who took this occasion to consult the young man on the interests of the united settlements, and to commission him to transact various matters of business touching those interests, as soon as he should arrive in London. In order that Christopher should receive due attention at the Office of Plantations, and have immediate access to Privy Councillors and other official personages whom he was directed to approach, Sir William Stapleton provided him with credentials and letters of introduction that gave him, in the official coteries of Charles the Second's London, the status of a political envoy from the Captain-General of the Leeward Islands.

Having sailed from St. Kitt's on 12 July, 1682, Christopher arrived in London on the seventeenth day of the following September, after a tedious and comparatively uneventful passage.

CHAPTER XII.

CHANNELL ROW, WESTMINSTER.

Charles Brett's Death—His Parentage and Office at Court—His Interment and Mural Tablet in St. Margaret's Church, Westminster—The Name and Neighbourhood of Channell Row—The Letter-Writer's London Address—Tokens and Token-Drinking—The Token-Feast at the Sun Tavern—Constantine Phipps of Gray's Inn—Edward Thorn Unmasked—His Profligate Life in St. Christopher's Island—Colonial Morality.

A GREAT disappointment awaited Christopher on his return to the mother-country. His intercourse with his brother-in-law, Charles Brett, was singularly affectionate, and was attended with every sign of mutual confidence. Whilst employing his cousin, William Poyntz, to execute commissions in the city, and trusting his cousin, John Jeaffreson of Clopton, to manage his Suffolk property, Christopher had made Charles Brett his attorney-in-chief, with power to act for him in all matters in England during his sojourn in the West Indies. And of all his old comrades, Charles Brett was the man whom Christopher was most eager to grasp by the hand, as he made his slow passage up the Thames. It caused him no common grief to be greeted, on landing at the docks, with the announcement that his dear friend Charles had been dead just sixteen weeks.

The only son of Major-General Brett of Rotherby in Leicester, some time Governor of the Isle of Wight, by Frances, daughter of Sir Henry Neville of Billingbeere, county Berks, Charles Brett was for many years a Gentleman Pensioner in ordinary to Charles the Second, and held that office at court up to the time of his death, which took place on 24 May, 1682, in the fifty-first year of his age, when he was interred in his parish church of St. Margaret, Westminster,* hard by the old Abbey, in which he had married Christopher's only sister on 3 March, 1673-4.

Taking coach from the docks to Westminster, Christopher drove over the rugged pavements of Fleet Street and the Strand, and made good speed to his sister's house in Channell Row, midway between the Abbey and Whitehall. And that house he made his London residence till his sister's second

---

* The Mural Tablet, placed to his memory in St. Margaret's Westminster, has been removed from its original position, but it is still preserved in one of the vestibules of the Church. After noticing his first wife Anne, the daughter of Sir Ambrose Browne, first Baronet, of Beechworth Castle, co. Surrey, the legend of this monument describes his second wife and widow as " Mary, daughter of Colonel Jeaffreson of Dullingham in Cambridgeshire." In the registration of the lady's marriage, the lady's name is misspelt "Mary Jefferson."—*Vide*, "Westminster Abbey Registers."—She married, 2ndly, Mr. Lewis of Glamorganshire, (mentioned in the ensuing letters), whom she survived; and after making a third and unhappy marriage with Mr. Morgan, a gentleman of the Principality, she died s. p. in 1703, on 30 June, in which year Letters of Administration, " de bonis non," were granted to her brother on the estate of her first husband, Charles Brett.

marriage with Mr. Lewis, of Glamorganshire.

Whether antiquaries are justified in saying that Channell was a corruption of cannon, and that the Row took its name from the canons of the adjacent abbey, may be questioned; but it is certain that the thoroughfare still called Cannon Row was the same street in which Madam Brett lived for several years, and that it was ordinarily designated Channell Row in the days of the two Charles's. It is Channell Row in Howell's "Letters" and in "The Hind and Panther Transversed:"—

> "What wretch would nibble on a hanging shelf,
> When at Pontacks he may regale himself?
> Or to the House of cleanly Rhenish go,
> Or that at Charing Cross or that at Channel Row?
> "*The Hind and Panther Transversed.*"

Few streets of old Westminster had a better reputation than Channell Row with the gallants and belles of Charles the Second's London. Consisting for the most part of snug cosy houses, inhabited by *attachés* to Whitehall, the Row was in the very heart of society. The King's Palace, the Hall of

Justice, Charing Cross, the Abbey and St. James's Park were all within three minutes' walk of its watchman's box. Betwixt two April showers a lady, living in Channell Row, could trip with dry feet and feathers from her own door to morning service in the Abbey or to the afternoon promenade in Westminster Hall. She could slip by any one of six secret alleys from her own door to a friend's lodgings in Whitehall. If it came on to rain, when she was in the Mall or the Spring Gardens, a chair or coach would take her home in less than a minute. Her street was "the Row" for fashionable *flâneurs*, as much as the booksellers' street hard-by St. Paul's Churchyard was "the Row" for poets and pedants. Everyone in the fashionable world knew Channell Row, and Channell Row knew everything about everyone in the fashionable world. Instead of suffering in character from its close proximity to two large and much frequented taverns, Channell Row was indebted for much of its prestige to the presence of the Old Rhenish House and the Mum House.

"The tavern" was in the seventeenth century what "the club" is now-a-days to gentlemen of the town; and a man of fashion in Charles the Second's London was delighted to tell his friends that he lived next door to a public-house that did a roaring trade. The letters, which the Penny Post brought to Christopher during his residence in the Row after his return from the West Indies, were directed thus:—

These
For Captain Jeaffreson,
At Madame Bretts,
In Channell Row,
Neare ye Mum-House,
Westminster.

Whence it may be inferred that if the young man did not insist on his military rank and require the world to recognize it, his friends deemed it the part of politeness to have regard to his martial quality.

Having entered into possession of his quarters in Channell Row, and condoled with his sister on her loss of an excellent husband, Christopher took early days to deliver the many letters which his friends in the Leeward Islands had charged him to convey to their friends in England. He was no less prompt in delivering to Constantine Phipps the tokens sent him for festal purposes by his brother, Captain James Phipps, of St. Christopher's Island, and the tokens sent by Captain Pogson, a planter of the same island, to his two sons, apprentices boarding in the house of their master, Mr. Wrayford, West Indian Merchant, of Bow Lane.

Gifts of money, to be spent at their discretion for their own pleasures, the tokens for the two boys were mere "tips." But the tokens of fraternal affection for Constantine Phipps require a word of explanation.

In the seventeenth century it was usual for a man, withdrawn by circumstances from a circle of attached friends, to send on convenient occasions to any one of the "old set" a present of money to defray the charges of a festal meeting, at which the members of the *coterie* would commemorate the virtues and drink to the health of the founder of

K 2

the feast. Sometimes the gift was only enough for "glasses all round," in which case the consumers of the token dispersed half-an-hour after they had met by appointment at a convenient tavern. Sometimes the gift was large enough to cover the cost of a grand dinner, followed by a drinking-bout. But more often it greatly exceeded the cost of "glasses round" in a bar-parlour, without amounting to a sufficient sum for a stately and luxurious repast. In this case, it was usual for the trustee of the token or tokens to summon the old friends to a token-feast, with an announcement that there would be "a whip" for supplementary expenses. Whilst social etiquette authorized a gentleman to offer this pecuniary complaisance to his distant friends, no sentiment of pride or delicacy prevented the haughtiest gentlemen from accepting a bounty that would now-a-days be regarded as an insult rather than a courtesy.

The tokens sent by Captain James Phipps amounted to such a sum that Constantine Phipps, one of the gayest students and smartest dancers in the Inns of Court, lost no time in sending out invitations for a family gathering at the Sun Tavern behind the Royal Exchange. Young Constantine Phipps (the future Lord Chancellor of Ireland, and the cousin of the inventor of the diving-bell) and Christopher Jeaffreson were brothers by affinity, and the dinner-party consisted chiefly of Phippses. Mr. Francis Phipps and Mr. and Mrs. Thomas Phipps Phipps came with Mr. and Mrs. Jackson and Mr. Langford. Her dress and state of sorrow forbade Mrs. Brett to join the party, which was a sumptuous and successful affair. The caterer exceeded the sum of the tokens, but as the feast was in Christopher's honour, he was not permitted to contribute a single coin to "the whip."

But the pleasure which Christopher experienced in greeting his former comrades and near relations, was disturbed by an incident which revealed to him the knavish genius and propensities of the man to whom he had entrusted his West Indian interest for five years.

Having ordered a new riding-coat of a London tailor named Penney, Christopher had not been many days in London before he entered the tradesman's shop, and learnt from Mrs. Penney how her husband had been defrauded by a young man named Edward Thorn, agent for a West Indian planter bearing the same name as Mr. Penney's new customer. Was it possible that the new customer knew aught of Edward Thorn? Continuing her story, the indignant dame explained how her husband had entrusted Edward Thorn with goods worth £35 or £40, to sell on commission in the Leeward Islands, and how Master Penney had never heard aught of his " venture" to the Indies, or received a single line from the fellow he had trusted to his sorrow.

Further inquiries about Mr. Thorn ascertained that, instead of having substantial " friends," he was a member of an indigent family, and that far from having connections who would entrust him with capital for his establishment in the West Indies, he had the ill word and opinion of everyone who knew him in London.

On making these discoveries, Christopher prepared himself to hear that he had no sooner sailed from St. Kitt's than Edward Thorn began to live after the wont of disorderly stewards to absentee proprietors.

Such intelligence reached England quickly.

Indeed, Christopher had not been back in London full twelve months before he knew from sure witnesses that Ensign Thorn, having displayed his true nature and thrown aside his disguise the instant his master had turned his back, was squandering his health and means in wild debauchery; that living at the rate of a £1,000 a-year, the cunning knave was spending more time in the hells and stews of Sandypoint than on his master's plantations, and that when he was "at home" he was surrounded with gamblers, drunkards, and wastrels. In so short a time Edward Thorn had by reckless riding killed four of his employer's best horses, and by wanton cruelty killed fourteen costly slaves.

This was pleasant news for the proprietor

who had engaged Mr. Thorn for five years, and could not discharge him till the end of that term without first proving that he had broken the chief articles of his contract. How could the master prove this? Where could he on the moment find another and less unsuitable agent?

He consoled himself by hoping that his good friends in St. Christopher's Island—the English gentlemen who wore swords and boasted of their noble ancestry, and daily drank their choice Madeira wine from silver cups adorned with armorial devices—would see that no further injury was done to his property. Three of those gentlemen, as overseers named in the indenture between the master and steward, had a right to supervise Mr. Thorn's proceedings. They had promised to inspect his accounts every year, and should his accounts exhibit any flagrant dishonesty, they had powers to remove him from his office. Under these circumstances, they would not fail to protect him from shameless despoliation.

Though he had spent more than five years

in the Leeward Islands, and had studied the immoral aspects and demoralizing influences of West Indian society, it did not occur to Christopher that whilst his closest friends in St. Christopher's Island would be more ready to wink at than punish his steward's misdemeanours, most of the gentlemen of the colony would for their private ends encourage the servant's dishonesty. Still further was he from imagining that a majority of his old acquaintances already regarded him as a mere absentee, and deemed it a good joke to see him plundered and defrauded.

CHAPTER XIII.

A COLONIAL COMMISSIONER IN DIFFICULTIES.

Failures in Lombard Street—Panic in the City—The Fall of Bantam—The Rye-House Plot—Mr. Blathwait's Services—Christopher's Petition to the King and Council for Soldiers—His Petition for Military Munitions—Success in the Council Chamber—Failure in the Department—Lord Dartmouth's Significant Speech—Christopher's Petition for an Allotment of Malefactors—Order of the Council respecting the same Petition—Corrupt Practices of the Gaoler of Newgate and the Recorder of London—Futile Contention with those Officers—Mr. Blathwait's Advice—Sir Leoline Jenkins's Intervention—Christopher's Speech to the Lords of the Council—His Defeat.

THE first year of Christopher's residence in Channell Row covered some important events. In London it was the year of Temple's failure in Lombard Street—a failure that caused a panic in the city and resulted in the ruin or embarrassment of several other bankers and merchants. It was also the year of the fall of Bantam to the Dutch, and of the Rye-House Plot, which last-named affair was regarded by Christopher as an incident favourable to his chances of getting some malefactors of a good quality for shipment to the Leeward Islands.

The letters of the year show that he was strenuous and importunate in his appeals to public and official men for the benefit of his particular colony. Having made the acquaintance of Mr. Blathwait, the Secretary of War, Clerk of the Privy Council, and Secretary to the Committee of Foreign Plantations, he was successful in his efforts to make that powerful man of affairs take an interest in the English Plantation of St. Christopher's Island. For a time the Secretary of Plantations overflowed with complaisance to Sir William Stapleton's envoy, and was at considerable pains to explain to him how he should proceed to get a consignment of malefactors, a fresh draft of soldiers, and a grant of warlike munitions, for his

West Indian settlement. Mr. Blathwait was also serviceable in introducing the political agent to the official people and great courtiers who could further his enterprises. Christopher saw the value of Mr. Blathwait's assistance; and in order that the colony might have the affectionate regard of so powerful a patron, he was urgent on the Assembly of St. Kitt's to make the Secretary of Plantations a handsome present.

In respect to his petition, in Sir William Stapleton's name, to the King and Council for a sufficient draft of soldiers to recruit the two companies of "regulars" on St. Christopher's Island, Christopher met with disappointment rather than success. For the application resulted in an order (dated 22 November, 1682) for thirty soldiers, instead of eighty or a hundred. But the envoy comforted himself with the assurance that the thirty soldiers would be picked men out of His Majesty's Guards, well-trained and well-equipt.

His petition, made in his own name, to

Charles the Second, for iron, cannon, shot, arms, and other ammunition for the new fort on Cleverly's Poynt in St. Christopher's Island, was read in Council on the 12 January, 1682-3, when it was so graciously received that the petitioner entertained sanguine hopes of good results. But when he went from the Council to the great officers on whom it devolved to give effect to the orders touching the petition, Christopher saw that success in the council-chamber might only be a prelude to defeat in the departments. At the Tower he was told in a significant manner by Lord Dartmouth that his colony could have all needful stores, provided it could pay for them. Mr. Blathwait in the blandest manner advised him not to expect too much, but to be content for the moment with a "few iron guns."

The alternate encouragements and disappointments which he encountered in his endeavours to obtain a grant of three hundred malefactors, sentenced to serve as slaves for eight years, should be observed with attention by the readers of his letters, which set forth with excellent clearness the conditions under which those bondsmen laboured in the plantations, as well as the terms on which they were transported and distributed amongst the planters, the way in which rival colonies competed for the grants of convict labour, and the circumstances which enabled the Recorder of London and the chief gaoler of Newgate to turn that rivalry to their profit.

The Lords of the Committee for Foreign Plantations having approved of his petition for three hundred malefactors, and the Lords of the Council having in consideration of that approval ordered that so many convicts should be consigned to the agent for St. Christopher's Island by the gaolers of gaols in London and Middlesex, Christopher was for a moment under the impression that it only remained for him to make arrangements for the safe transport of the prisoners, who would be consigned to him in lots of thirty or fifty persons from time to time. Inquiry soon caused him to fear he had taken too favourable a view of his case. Men of experience in such affairs assured him that, the order of the Council notwithstanding, he would not get a single lot of convicts until he had agreed to pay certain fees, varying from forty-five to fifty-five shillings for each malefactor, to the chief gaoler of Newgate, Captain Richardson. How this money would be divided the informants could not say precisely; but it was known that the greater part of each payment for a convict went into the pockets of Captain Richardson and the Recorder of London. Some of it went to the keepers of other London prisons, whose prisoners had been removed into Newgate; and there were gratuities paid out of each sum to under-gaolers and turnkeys.

There was no authority, but usage, for the exaction of these fees. The Privy Council had not sanctioned them. Probably the King and his nearest advisers knew nothing of the matter. Possibly the exactions were alike lawless and extortionate. Something, however, could be urged in their defence. Captain Richardson had given a prodigious sum for his office; the keepers of the other

London prisons had done likewise; and it was only fair that placemen should be repaid for their outlay in purchasing places of trust. It was also to the interest of society that the prison-keepers should have fees which stimulated them to take good care of the convicts on whose consignment to a colonial agent such fees were payable. In like manner, good came to society from a practice which encouraged the Recorder to exert himself for the conviction of scoundrels who might escape the grip of the law, if juries were not duly and cogently instructed to return verdicts of "guilty." Anyhow the fees must be paid. "No fee no convict" was law at the Old Bailey, even as "no song no supper" was law at the social table.

Christopher would have done better had he taken his friend's advice, and avoided a bootless contention with the two powerful officers. But he resolved to do his best to get the convicts, without paying the irregular fees.

Going to the Old Bailey on the day on which the next lot of convicts pleaded their pardons on condition of their transportation to the West Indies, and arriving there whilst the Lord Mayor and Sheriffs were still in court, he was putting in his demand for the convicts in accordance with the Council's order, that the next three hundred malefactors should be sent to St. Christopher's Island, when Captain Richardson stopt him with the announcement that all the just pardoned convicts had been disposed of. The agent for Jamaica had agreed to take the whole number, women and children as well as men, whereas Christopher had objected to take any but serviceable men. Consequently the agent for Jamaica would have the lot. St Kitt's must wait for the next gaol delivery.

Christopher went off in a fume to Mr. Blathwait, who received him with his invariable courtesy, and smiling in his sleeve advised him to go to Mr. Secretary (Sir Leoline) Jenkins. From Sir Leoline the agent for the St. Kitt's planters obtained neither redress nor reassurance. Mr. Secretary was disposed to think well of the arrangement which had been made. Possibly there was an irregularity in giving the preference to Jamaica over St. Kitts; but as the Jamaica people had taken women and children as well as men, had paid the clearance fees, signed the requisite bonds, and victualled a ship for their gaol-birds, it would be scarcely fair to deprive them of their cargo. But Christopher was not to be set aside in this manner; and as he declared his purpose of carrying the matter before the Council, Sir Leoline yielded so far as to write a letter to Captain Richardson, which forbade the delivery of the prisoners till the gaoler should receive further instructions.

A few days later the affair came before the Lords of the Council, who in the seventeenth century used to trouble themselves about contemptibly trivial matters. On the one hand their lordships were implored by the Jamaica merchants to allow them to carry out the malefactors consigned to them in the ordinary way by the judge and magistrates of the Old Bailey Court. On the other hand, their lordships were entreated to stand by their own mandate, which should have been obeyed by the Criminal Court. Christopher made a speech in support of his prayer; Sir Leoline Jenkins, Sir Phillip Floyd, Lord Halifax, the Lord President, and the Attorney-General taking part in the discussion, which certainly was not deficient in warmth. For awhile it would have seemed to an uninitiated auditor that the victory would be to the agent for St. Christopher's Island, who spoke out boldly against Captain Richardson's corrupt practices, and his insolence in setting at nought the Council's order. But the gaoler's influence was too powerful with their lordships, who decided in favour of the Jamaica petitioners. For Christopher, there was no course but to wait for the next lot of available malefactors, and to take them on the best terms he could make with the gaoler and the recorder.

Such were the matters in which the letter-writer interested himself for the sake of his colony, whilst diverting himself with the gaieties and humours of Charles the Second's town.

CHAPTER XIV.

ANOTHER YEAR OF SERVICE.

The hard Winter of 1683-4—Frost Fair—Prevalence of Small Pox—Death Rate of the Capital—" Mourning" the Fashionable Dress—Deaths of Sir Edward Brett and Colonel Gamiell—Intrigues and Competitors for Sir William Stapleton's Office—Christopher's exertions for his Colony—His First Shipment of Malefactors to St. Christopher's Island—He is appointed London Agent for his Colony—He presents Addresses to the King and the Duke of York on their Preservation from the Rye House Conspiracy—His Second Marriage—He moves from Channell Row to Cornhill.

THE winter of 1683-4 afforded Londoners the spectacle of a fair held for several successive weeks on the Thames; and in two of the letters written during that rigorous season, we have a vivid picture of the diversions of Frost Fair. At the same time small pox was so prevalent throughout the town, that it was scarcely less operative than the extreme cold in raising the bills of mortality to two hundred deaths per week. So fatal a winter could not be recalled by men of old age and clear memory. In the churches it was observed that two-thirds of every congregation wore black. At public gatherings bright colours were so rare that a gaudy costume attracted general attention. Though Christopher's health endured the rigour without injury, he did not escape the sorrow which pestilence or frost brought to every mansion and cabin of the capital. Whilst several of his friends were swept away by the epidemic, his father-in-law Colonel Gamiell and his old friend Sir Edward Brett perished from the keen north wind.

His letters show that throughout this memorable winter and the ensuing months till the middle of September, Christopher was a vigilant observer of public affairs, and plied his pen busily for the information of his West Indian friends. Everything in the way of European news was welcome to them; and in addition to the scraps of continental intelligence for which they had an insatiable appetite, Christopher sent them piquant notes touching the ambitions and dolitical intrigues of the various aspirants for the office of Captain-General of the Leeward Islands, which it was assumed Sir William Stapleton would resign on his arrival in England.

At the same time, Christopher was incessantly stirring in official quarters for the execution of the Council's grant of malefactors to his colony. Never a week passed in which he failed to refresh the memory of Mr. Blathwait. One month he was memorializing the Council, the next saw him in conference with the Commissioners for Foreign Plantations. His importunity and tact at length had their reward; and he had the satisfaction of sending off from the Thames to the West Indies a cargo of malefactors, after paying prison fees for them to the sum of forty-five shillings a head, just ten shillings less than the usual sum. Having obtained this small advantage by an infinite amount of wrangling, Christopher came to the conclusion that the game was not worth the candle, and that it would be better henceforth to purchase the good will of the gaoler and the recorder by submitting to their extortions.

In this same year, Christopher's exertions for his colony were acknowledged by the colonists in the manner most acceptable to his feelings. With the consent and approval of Sir William Stapleton, the Governor and Council of the English colony of St. Kitt's appointed him to act as their Political Agent; and together with the letter which announced his selection for this appointment, the Governor and Council sent him their congratulatory addresses to His Majesty the King and His Royal Highness the Duke of York, on their preservation from the Rye House conspiracy, requesting him to present the same to the Sovereign and his brother. When he announced the execution of this task, Christopher acknowledged his receipt of the honorarium of £50 sent him by the

Governor and Council, and declared his intention to spend it for the advantage of the colony.

With the close of his second year in town, the letter-writer's residence in Channell Row came to an end.

After spending more than two years in widowhood, Madam Brett was married, on 11 September, 1684, to " Mr. Lewis, a gentleman of good estate and family in Glamorganshire," who agreed that he and his wife should retain the house in Channell Row as their town residence, and should divide their time between Westminster and Wales, " spending the winter in towne and the summer in the country."

On this event (which occasioned him the liveliest satisfaction) Christopher retired from Channell Row, and gave directions that his letters should be addressed to him at the house of his cousin, William Poyntz, in Cornhill.

To Christopher, a residence in the city was as convenient as a residence in the purlieus of the Court; for his time was divided equally between Whitehall (where he idled with his sister's set of friends, whilst lying in wait for the official personages who could help his colony) and the city coffee-houses, where he drank Madeira and smoked tobacco with the merchants and captains and hangers-on of the West Indian interests.

CHAPTER XV.

THE LAST OF THE MEMOIR.

Charles the Second's Death—James the Second's Accession—Argyll's Insurrection—French Refugees—The last Year's Letters—How they should be read—Notable Scenes—The Malefactors' March—Governor Hill's Breach of Contract—How Mr. Vickers kept his Word—American Smartness—West Indian Morality.

THE next two years of Christopher's life were crowded with incidents of historical moment. Charles the Second's death, and his brother's peaceful accession to the throne were followed quickly by Argyll's rebellion in Scotland, and Monmouth's rising in the West of England. Trials ensued in rapid succession; and when the culprits of high degree had paid the penalty of failure, justice did her stern work on inferior rebels. Compassion for the victims of Monmouth's rashness was followed by the deeper and more general commiseration for the French Protestants, who, on the revocation of the Edict of Nantes, fled to England under circumstances that made them grateful recipients of a frigid charity.

All these matters, and hundreds of incidents that resulted from them, are noticed in the letters which Christopher sent to his correspondents in St. Christopher's Island. From the fullness and regularity of these despatches, it may be inferred that, as Political Agent for the English colony, he was under an obligation of honour or interest to send its Governor and Members of Council such intelligence respecting English politics and Continental affairs, as he could gather in the coffee-houses of the City and the anterooms of Ministers. To realize the interest with which his letters were perused by Governor Hill, the modern reader should compare them with the scrappy Gazettes and Intelligencers that accompanied them to the West Indies, and observe how large a proportion of their more interesting news relates to matters about which the printed journals are altogether silent. His picture of the Thames, as it appeared when Monmouth and Grey were brought by water to Whitehall; his description of the battle of Sedgemoor, or Bridgewater it was christened whilst the dead still lay unburied on the battle-field; his account of the Duke's execution on Tower Hill; his sketch of Lord Delamere's trial in Westminster Hall; and his comprehensive report of the proceedings of the Ecclesiastical Commissioners, when they tried the Bishop of London for his conduct in the matter of Doctor Sharp, Rector of St. Giles's-in-the-Fields, may be mentioned as examples of the freedom and fullness with which the private correspondent wrote about subjects which the scribes of public newsletters avoided or misrepresented.

Moreover, for their proper enjoyment, the letters should be read now as they were read by the gentlemen of St. Christopher's Island, two hundred years since. To apprehend their original value and piquancy, one must read not only the lines, but *between* the lines, and seize the meaning of hints. When the correspondent announced in concise terms recent changes at the Council Table, and in the Army, Navy, Law, and Church, Governor Hill could make his own comments on the facts. In like manner, the Governor had no need of editorial explanations when he read of rumoured changes in the same departments of the State. When Christopher wrote that he would not sell his West Indian property, as he could imagine that at a not very remote time he might gladly avail himself of so peaceful a retreat from troubles, his correspondent knew right well what troubles were indicated.

At the same time, the special correspondent was on the alert to promote the material interests of his colony, and take measures for the protection of his own estate in it. In his written instructions for the ejectment of Edward Thorn from his property, and the careful letters of guidance and counsel which he penned to the gentleman who succeeded that fraudulent scapegrace in the stewardship of his West Indian interests, the writer is seen in the character of an enterprising, discreet, energetic man of business. Other glimpses of him, when acting in the same character, are afforded by epistles that relate to the public business of the colony rather than to his private affairs. In one of them, he is seen and heard before the Lords Commissioners of Trade, defending himself with equal spirit and ability against the ungenerous imputations of Lord Keeper North. In another, he appears as the chief actor in as droll a street-scene of Old London as any preserved to us by the gossiping chroniclers of London in the days of the later Stuarts.

Mindful of his obligation to hold the rascals in custody, and of the heavy forfeiture to which he was liable should any of them escape, Christopher was himself the captain of the volunteer guard that conducted thirty-nine malefactors, shortly after six o'clock on the Easter Eve of 1685, from Newgate to London Bridge, where they went on board the barges that conveyed them to the convict-ship. Heavily manacled, and surrounded by a strong military escort, the bare-footed culprits had no chance of escape, but their hard and desperate case could not break their courage or extinguish their delight in mischief. A crowd, of course, gathered round the captives and the guard, and it happened several times during the march from the prison to the river that a well-dressed idler, whose curiosity had impelled him to go too near the gang, was caught by a fettered hand, and in a trice stripped of hat and periwig, amidst the uproarious acclamations of the spectators.

In respect to the terms and circumstances under which these convicts and a previous lot of malefactors were transported to St. Christopher's Island, the reader should observe how the agent for the colony was treated by his co-adventurers, Governor Hill and Mr. Vickers.

The convicts were transported on the joint responsibility and joint risk of Governor Hill, Mr. Vickers, and Christopher. Governor Hill was a soldier, who had distinguished himself on European battle-fields, and lived in the best sets of Charles the Second's court, before he went out to the Leeward Islands to succeed Colonel Matthews as the English Governor of St. Kitt's; and Mr. Vickers was one of the chief planters of the island. By these gentlemen and Christopher it was agreed that all the sugar, paid in lieu of money for the convicts by their purchasers in the island, should be shipped to London for sale; and that, after the charges for the transportation of the malefactors had been deducted from the proceeds of the sale, the residue should be divided into three equal portions and distributed amongst the partners. Besides undertaking to advance the money for prison fees and other expenses of the venture, Christopher promised to take upon himself all the trouble of receiving the prisoners, and putting them on board-ship, provided his companions in the venture would be at the trouble of disposing of the cargo in the West Indies.

The way in which Governor Hill and Mr. Vickers broke faith with their friend in respect to this compact is significant of the state of West Indian morality. On the arrival of the malefactors in St. Christopher's Island, the two adventurers on the spot first selected the best men for service on their own plantations, paying of course the stipulated amount of sugar for them. That done, Governor Hill and his confederate allowed the other planters on the spot to take their pick of the live-stock; the weakly, and aged, and sick malefactors being consigned to the plantations of the absent comrade, who had, of course, supposed that his friends, even if they looked out for themselves first, would make his interest their next concern.

When the purchase sugar for the malefactors had been delivered to the vendors in the usual way of *business*, instead of shipping it to London in accordance with their agreement, Governor Hill and Mr. Vickers took another course. First Mr. Vickers took his share, or what he was pleased to think his proper share, of the sweet-stuff, and then Governor Hill took possession of

VOL. I. M

the residue, on an undertaking to divide it equally between himself and his absent friend, who had furnished the requisite funds for the venture. The case would have been bad, had Colonel Hill shipped at the earliest opportunity to Christopher one-third of the deposited sugar, together with such an additional quantity as would cover the expenses which Christopher had incurred for the joint enterprise; but the breach of trust and contract was far more flagrant, for not a pound of the sugar was sent to the letter-writer when several months had passed since Colonel Hill and Mr. Vickers divided the stock. Again and again Christopher wrote to Colonel Hill, expostulating against the way in which he was treated, and begging, as though he were asking a favour, that at least he might not be kept any longer out of his right.

One is apt to speak of the sharp practice and impudent frauds of New York adventurers, as moral phenomena that show how greatly the modern Americans have degenerated in respect of probity and honour from their English progenitors. The Old World likes to persuade itself, and succeeds in persuading itself, that the new has a financial immorality of its own invention, which may be regarded as a fair example of the depraving influence of republican institutions.

Christopher's letters, however, abound with evidence that West Indian society in the seventeenth century exhibited the same propensities that distinguish the least scrupulous and most adventurous of our American cousins at the present time. The conclusion may wound our national pride, and be especially offensive to those who like to express their abhorrence of Transatlantic corruption and dishonesty, but the observant and candid reader of the ensuing epistles will admit that American "smartness" has a pedigree of considerable antiquity, and may be traced to the planters of our earliest settlements in the New World.

There is little to be said respecting the letter-writer's career after the date of the last letter of this collection. It does not appear from any of the later documents of his writing how long he continued to act in London as agent for the English Colony of St. Christopher's Island. Whilst there is no evidence that he ever revisited the Leeward Islands, some of his letters, written in the earlier years of the eighteenth century, countenance the opinion that he never returned to the West Indian property, which yielded an increasing revenue under the management of Mr. Sedgwick, (who proved an equally competent and honest steward,) and in still later time fully repaid the labour and money expended in its re-settlement. On the other hand, it is certain that he passed the greater part of his time, during the reigns of William the Third, Anne, and George the First, at his manor-house in Cambridgeshire, where he distinguished himself by the zeal with which he discharged the various duties of a county magistrate and a country gentleman, and died on August 1, 1725, in the seventy-fifth year of his age.

Part II.

THE VOYAGE TO THE WEST-INDIES

AND THE

LETTERS FROM ST. CHRISTOPHER'S ISLAND.

CHAPTER I.

OUTWARD BOUND.

(16 *Feb.* 167⅚ *to* 24 *May,* 1676,)

The Writer's Desire to visit St. Christopher's Island—He takes Leave of his Friends in Billingsgate—Gravesend — Margaret Road — Plymouth — Catwater — Windbound Ships—The Deserts Islands—Madeira—Funchial—Curious Superstitions and Religious Usages—The Enchanted Island—The Canary Islands—Flying Fish, Dolphins and Bunnitoes—A Gale—Descade, Guadaloupe and Antigua—Hospitable Entertainment at Mountserrat—Nevis—St. Christopher's Island.

[The following narrative of the writer's Voyage from the Thames to St. Christopher's Island (16 Feb. 167⅚ to 24 May, 1676) was written by himself in the Letter-Book, where it is entitled—" The Voyage of St. Christophers in the West Indies."—J. C. J.]

MY inclinations from my very infancy leading me to travell, and having passed two yeares of my nonage in France (which tyme I spent in seeing the most remarqueable things of that kingdome, as well as in learning the language); and some few yeares after my retourne to England, my desier of seeing the Island of St. Christophers (which tooke beginning in me before age had given me the capacity of travelling) now increasing in me, I tooke a resolution to forsake friends and relations, towne and country, to settle as well as see an interest, with which it had pleased our good God to blesse my father upon that island, who was pleased amongst other things to bequeath it to me, to whom he had given the name of the isle.

In pursuance of my designe, upon the sixteenth of February, $167\frac{5}{6}$, takeing leave of most of my friends at Billingsgate, I went from London to Graves-end in company with my sister, brother Brett, and two or three friends more only; and the seventeenth beeing thursday, about seven of the clock in the evening, I went on board the 'Jacob and Mary,' a vessell of about a hundred and fifty tunns, 14 or 16 gunns, a square stearne, with good accommodations for myselfe and servants, which were but four in number. The master's name was Andrew Vandevell.

About eight of the clock, we got under saile, the winde blowing softly at South West.

Sunday the 20th, we came to anchor in Margarett Road, and the next day in the downes, where we went ashoar; but the wind in two or three dayes promessing faire for vs, we staid no longer there, where there is little or nothing that is worthy to be noted, only the three castles, which serve more for defence than ornament to the place.

Saturday the 26th, the windes being contrary we put into Plymouth, where we rode at anchor in Catwater tenne dayes, in which tyme we had the opportunety of seeing the Royall Fort, built by his majestie that now is, and allsoe the towne.

The sixth of March, the winde comeing about to the North East, in the afternoone we hoisted sayle and stood out to sea, in company with many other shipps, that had leyen winde-bounde with vs, with whom we soon parted, only excepting one small vessell of fourty or 50 tunn, that kept vs company for a tyme; one Mr. Needles master.

The tenth day it blew hard, which made a verry rough and hollow sea, which raked vs fore and aft, breakeing sometymes over our quarter; in which great seas, our shipp's crew concluded, that our little leakie companion was buried.

The 13th and 14th, we ley becalmed.

The 15th the wind blew fresh in our teeth, which continued until the twentieth, with some little variation; but, then the windes proveing more favourable, the 28th we came in sight of the Islands called "the deserts," and the same evening we espied a sayle, which we doubted was a Turke; which made us putt ourselves in a posture of defence, and the next morning, findeing that he had chased vs all night, we were confirmed in our opinions, and seeing that he made still all the sayle he could after vs, we prepared all things for a fight, and continued in that posture all the day and night;

and the next day, drawing neare the Island of the Madera, our pursuer quitted his chase, and we got into Funchiall road in the afternoone; where wee were verry neare loosing our shippe, the master being unacquainted, and comeing too boldely in near the shoar, in a daingerous place. But the men towed her off againe; and Mr. Needles, who we feared had beene lost, was got in before vs, two or three dayes, and came then on board vs, adviseing the master where to anchor, and that it was not safe for him to goe ashoar at the towne, but at some distance from it, where, with difficultie and not without being well wetted, we got ashoar, and went to Mr. Pickford and Mr. Allen's, the consull's house, to whom the shippe was consigned; where we met with civill entertainment from those persons, whose repute as well as gravety gave weight to their wordes.

We understood that this island is eighteene leagues long and seven broad, containing fourscore thousand inhabitants, produceing some years twenty-five thousand pipes of wine, besides sugar and corne, with which it doth not sufficiently fournish its people, who are supplied from England and elsewhere, as allso for herrings, pilchards, beefe, mutton, baizes, perpetuanas, hatts, and the like, which are there bartered for wine and sweetmeats. The towne or cittie of Funchial is beautified with lofty stone houses and churches, especially that which stands upon the place or greene, which is enriched with eleven large altars, sumptuously guilded, and more particularly the high altar set forth with neat pictures, imagery, and with other ornaments, pleasant to the eye, if not abused by idolatry. The cannopy over this altar is richely guilded and carved, and likewise the pillers that support it. The seats of the singeing men are likewise curiously carved.

This island by geographers is laid down as in Affrica. It belongs to the king of Portugall, whose subjects, togeather with a mixt race of free negroes, mullatos, and mustees, are the possessors and inhabitants thereof. It lyes in thirty-two degrees, odde minutes, north latitude. The king of Portugall sends over a new governour every three yeares; and during the tyme we were there, this triennial chainge happened. The Porteguise fleete, of 13 or 14 saile with their convoy, brought the new governour, who, with a bishop bound with part of the fleet for Angola, the other part being designed for Brazile, was courteously received ashoar; the three forts fireing their guns (which forts, standing at convenient distances along the shoar, beautifie the towne), and also a fort, which stands upon a rock, a small distance from the land, between which and the shoar, the Porteguise ships ride in outwindes. For when the windes blow in upon the land, the sea rises, and the road is so daingerous, that other vessells, that are not sheltered by the said rocks, are forced to stand out to sea, for fear of being driven ashoar. This fort allso fired its guns, which were but few. The townsmen were in armes, and there were severall ceremonies, joyned with feasting, adjoyning to the Douane or Custom House, which is a loftie faire structure, in a large paved court, where the merchants walk as upon an Exchainge, and where are several guns planted: it pointeing out towards the sea.

Funchiall is the only cittie upon the island, which is verry high land. The tops of the mountains are usually manteled with clouds. The walkes from the cittie are so rugged and uneven, that one may be sayd to climbe rather than walke abroad. But these difficulties are recompensed with the fruitefull, well cultivated, and pleasant viniards, the frequent delightfull landskipps, with the frequent and odoriferous scents of the weedes or common herbes and field-flowers, which Nature produces of herselfe in the barren and unmanured parts of this most pleasant and fruitfull spot; where neither the extreame colde of winter, nor the violent heat of summer pinches or scorches the inhabitants. Only, as in England the sun in summer is thought too powerfull, so heere, but not to that degree, as may be imagined.

Not farre from the cittie are too famous nunnerys; the one called Sancta Clara, in which are three hundred nuns; the other of the Incarnation, in which are seventy-three nuns. These women vse more freedome then ever I could observe or heare of amongst any of theire profession in France. For not only the young gentlemen of the island, but wee, that were straingers, were permitted to converse with them at one nunnery through a grate; but at the other, the dore beeing opened, there was nothing but the threshold, which neither they nor wee were permitted to passe over.

We understood but little of their language, but made a shift to barter some ribbands for sweetmeats. They seemed verry pleasant and free in their discourses; but, an honourable cleargyman appearing, the doores were shutt. He went up a payer of staires, followed by severall young gentlemen, who, as we supposed, were admitted to the speeche of the Lady Abbesse. But we durst not intrude. Wee were tould of two other nunnerys, which wee did not see, from one of which all the nuns were runaway. It was called the Convent of Converted. There is likewise, in or neare the cittie, a convent of Franciscan Fryers and a College of Jesuites, which is not quite built; the worke beeing, as it is saydd, delayed, because the king allowes them yearely a certaine some of money untill the same be finished, for the sake of which they are content to continue to delay the worke.

Every six or seven yeares, the king sends hither a judge who unravells all causes, that have not been well decided in that tyme, before whom appeales lye, imposing fines and penalties upon such as merit them; and so he retournes home.

Raines are sometymess much wanted by the islanders, for which theire idols or images of their saints suffer most severely, by severall sorts of chastisements, and are brought into the cittie, and carried otherwhiles in prosession. Trying foule meanes as well as faire, if they wont heare theire prayers, the islanders try if beateing will learne them better manners; like Baalls priests, who leaped and stamped on the altar, when theire deaf God would not heare.

The habits of the people are various: something conformable to the modes of the nations they trade with. They weare daggers and long swords, and are used to stabb one another in the night unawares.

There are many discourses here of an Inchanted Island, that at several tymes haith beene visibly seene by the people of this island, (which though it may seeme too fabulous to impose on the beliefe of incredulous persons), I shall relate what wee had from not a few most credible persons of that place; who in a serious manner assured us that, to the Northward or North-Westward of this island, appeared land at divers tymes, and not only to the islanders, but allso to shipps at sea, that at one tyme it was seene for a moneths tyme togeather, and an other tyme for a fortnight, and then the Governour employed a French shippe, which went out upon the discovery, but he could never finde it. That such reports are no novelties, wittnesse the seamen's Platts, in which are layd downe severall Islandes (as I have observed) which are yet undiscovered, though it is sayd they have been seene and named by ships, passeing that way every yeare, going or comeing from the West Indies.

But now it is tyme to retourne to the seaside, where it flowes six foot, and from whence, our vessell haveing taken in her wines, we went on board, the consull affording vs his company; where, after some tyme, he tooke leave of vs. But the winde being scant, we waited untill the next day, which being the thirteenth in the afternoone, about five of the clocke, the winde bloweing off shoar, we got undersayle, and stoode out to sea; where we mett with a brisque North and by West gaile which, by the 15th day at seven in the morning, brought us in sight of Palma, one of the Canary Islandes, where we parted againe with Mr. Needles (who sayled allso out of the Maderas in company with vs), we stearing our course more to the westward, the winde being now more favourable, and come to the Eastward of the North.

Tuesday the eighteenth, we passed about nine of the clocke that latitude, called the tropick of Cancer; and for feare of calmes we stood away due South and by West, untill we had run out our westing, thinkeinge it strange that all this tyme we saw no fishe except it were flying fish, (which, though common at sea may be a subject of wonder to such as are home-bred). This fish, no bigger than a small herring, are chased by the dolphins and bunnitoes, to whom their slow motion in the water would inevitably make them a prey, had not nature or rather providence supplied the deffect by giving them wings, with which they fly in whole shoales, but not very farre, for no sooner are their wings dry, but they drop into theire element, the water. It is usual for them to fly into the shipps. We had one or two come on board our vessell.

The 24th, we had the sun directly in our zenith; but a fresh gale made vs not sensible of any inconvenience by its heat.

Monday the eighth of May, about six of the clocke in the evening, the setting sun discovered to us the island of Descada; which was a welcome sight to us, who were forced to keepe the pump goeing night and day, by reason of a dangerous leake we had sprung at sea, which we could not finde, and which increasing would have soone beene too much for us, if bad weather had kept us at sea. Having passed Descada in the night, and on the contrary side to what our master intended, the next morning we run along near Guardeloup and Antegoa, and in the evening near Montserratt, where we lay severall dayes, and where we were entertained civilly by Deputy-Governor Carroll, Colonel Reade's widdow, Captain Hodges, Captain Bromley, and Mr. Liddall, with severall others. This is a pleasant and fruitfull land, verry rockie but a sandy soyle; the wayes uneven and in some parts dangerous. The inhabitants are mostly Irish, the better sort English. The two townes, between which our vessell rode at anchor are called Plimouth and Kingsale, which is the windermost. These two nations accord not upon this island. The Irish are most malicious against the English. The surf running very high we were detained here, and the more for that our boat was stayed, as the Deputy-Governour was intended to goe on board vs.

The 20th, in the evening, having passed 13 or 16 days there, we parted from thence leaving that island in al-larme at the sight of five sayle of ships.

The next day, being Sunday the 21st, we came to anchor at Nevis, and went on shoar at Charles-towne in the afternoone; where Mr. Helmes, the merchant to whome the shippe was consigned, conducted us (the Generall not being upon the island), to Colonel Russells, the Governour's, where I remayned three days, and was most courteously entertayned.

The 24th, I hired a shalloope, and with my goods and servants arrived that night at St. Christopher's.

CHAPTER II.

THE FIRST YEAR IN ST. CHRISTOPHER'S ISLAND.

(24 *May* 1676 *to* 11 *November* 1676).

A West-Indian ' Store'—Trade in the Leeward Islands—
The Islanders' favourite Wine—Want of Artisans—
'Honest' Mr. Worley—Indigo and Sugar—The Writer
turns Planter—Apprehensions of War—Poverty of the
Planters—Goods most needed by them—The Writer's
Sugar-Work—A West-Indian Agent in London—French
Planters—Their Jealousy and Insolence—Lady Stapleton—Sir William Stapleton, Captain-General of the
' Leeward Islands'—Extent and Boundaries of the
Writer's Plantations.

LETTER I.

To the Writer's Cousin, Mr. William Poyntz, Upholder,
at the Sign of ' the Goat' in Cornhill, near the Royal
Exchange, London.

[*Note.*—Mr. Poyntz, the upholsterer of
Cornhill, was a grandson of Aden Parkyns,
Esq., Co. Nottingham, whose nephew Colonel
Isham Parkyns of Bonney (or Bunney) Park,

in that county was the royalist defender of Ashby-de-la-Zouche against the Parliament. Notice should be taken of the writer's allusion to the terms of trade in the West Indies, where dealers in every kind of commodity were expected to take payment in kind, and also to give long credit. Having trucked their English exports for wine at Madeira, Merchant Adventurers from London trucked their pipes of Madeira wine at St. Christopher's for sugar, tobacco, or indigo. When the ladies of the Leeward Islands bought silks and ribands at Colonial stores, they paid for their purchases in the staple products of the islands. The planters of St. Kitts bought their horses and negroes with sugar, instead of money. At the same time, their free servants were content to take their wages in the same commodity.—J. C. J.]

St. Christopher's, June, 5 1676.

Dear Cousen,—I am now, thankes bee to God, arrived safe at St. Christopher, where I have exposed your goods to sale, togeather with my owne; but I finde the island in a much poorer condition than I expected. Insoemuch so, that there is little hope of vending any thing, but what necessity enforces people to become our chapmen for; and that I must give credit for to the rich as well as the poor, which I finde to bee altogether the custome of these isles. Nor have I received a pound of sugar nor of indigo (except of two or three persons), for all the sales, which I have made, which have been pretty considerable. . . . Your goods came by very little dammage, and some of them will I hope prove a good commoditie; but the trade being prohibited between the English and the French upon this island hinders the sale of dry commodities very much. But yet what does sell turnes to indifferent good accompt; insoemuch that I should be sorry to be forced to buy any thing here that I could be furnished with from Old England.

I promised to informe you what are the best commodities in these partes. I must begin with Madera wine, as the most profitable; for the merchant sends to that islande baizes, searges, that is perpetuanes, hatts, cheese, butter, white and red herrings, pilchards and beefe, all which, if they come to a bad market there, are good commodities here, but being trucked there for wines makes a double profitt of the voyage. And there is noe living here without those wines. Therefore, when any shipps are bound for those partes, and from thence hither, I desire you would make a small venture for mee, though it bee but for three or four pipes. If you consigne the goods to Mr. Pickfourd and Mr. Obediah Allen, I doubt not they will be just in shipping the valew for my use. It is worth sometimes five or seven pounds a pipe. If you can doe this with conveniency, it would save me the charge of buying it here. And if there bee more then enough for my own drinking I feare not to dispose of it well.

Whatsoever other goods you send mee, I desier you would shipp them if possible on vessels bound for this island; if not, directing to Nevis which is neare; but if she bee bounde to severall portes 'tis daingerous.

At Michelmas there will sett out another fleet for these portes, amongst which if there be any bound for this island, or if not, one that is bound for Nevis, I desire you would send a box of Castill soape, a chest of candells, two gray hatts fit for my owne wearing (well wrought, or else the sunne will make them flappe,) four more of an ordinary sort, halfe a dozen barrells of beefe, and a small case of drinking-glasses. Provisions are scarce here, and I was not well advised in not bringing with mee all that I write for now. . . . If you can procure me a carpenter or two, and one or two masons, they will bee very serviceable, if they bring their tooles with them. I pray you hearken out for such, and for a joyner, Suche servants are as golde in these partes. I desire you would act for me at home, as I do for you here, and I hope to give you satisfaction in what you have trusted mee with; and lett not this letter from a young merchant or rather poor planter (for soe I intende to bee) now, disincourage you. . . .

Your affectionate kinsman,
CHRISTOPHER JEAFFRESON.

LETTER II.

To the Writer's father-in-law, Colonell George Gamiell, London.

[*Note.*—The greater part of this letter relates to the defaults and dishonest behaviour of Mr. Worley, Member of the Legislative Assembly of St. Christopher's, and tenant of the writer's principal plantation in the island. Mr. Worley's neglect to pay his rent, and the reports of his general remissness in affairs of business were amongst the causes that determined the landlord to visit his West Indian property. In the with-held passages of the letter, the writer recounts the steps he has taken to get possession of the defaulter's personal estate, and protect himself from further loss from the bankrupt planter.—J. C. J.]

St. Christopher's, 5 June, 1676.

Honored Sir,—I am sorry to have noe better news to write you, and nothing but what I am confident will seeme to you, as it was, to mee astonishing; nor could I well credit it, till I found it too trew. At my first comeing into these parts, that is whilst I was at Mountserrat and Nevis, I could hear of nothing but the honesty and poverty of Mr. Worley. The last I found as trew as the former was false, which made mee loose no time to request an attachement from the governour to seize on his personal estate. . . . I finde everybody unwilling to act to Mr. Worley's prejudice; nor can I repose confidence in any man upon the island. Some raile at mee as one that is come to ruin Mr. Worley and the island, making his interest and the island's insepar- able, and they stick not to say that my plan- tation has ruined him. But most of them are conscious of some other misfortunes that have bin the reall cause of his miscarridge. As I have learned, Mr. Hezekiah Usher, a merchant of New England, sent him an accompt of six hundred pounds sterling, which hee, being illiterate, consented to rather then to have the concerne disputed. This way went most of his indigo. Besides he lost a ship at New England, and I am apt to believe his indigo of late has yielded him but small profit, because it doth now seldom thrive, and I see every body that is able, working upon sugar, which is a certaine gaine. But Mr. Worley is hardly capable of such an enterprise, though he hath put canes in the ground fifteen months since; but they are good for little. I intend now I am here to settle the plantation, though it cost mee a good some of money, as it certainely will doe; but I hope the advantage will answer it in the end, if wee have peace with the French, who are now much alarmed by the Dutch, who have taken Marygalante, and have, it is believed, a further designe in these partes...

  I reste, Sir,
   Your obedient son-in-law,
    CHRISTOPHER JEAFFRESON.

LETTER III.

To the Writer's cousin, Mr. William Poyntz, Upholder, at the sign of 'the Goat' in Cornhill, near the Royal Exchange, London.

[*Note.*—The passages, with-held from this letter, consist chiefly of repetitions of the instructions and orders given to Mr. Poyntz in the letter dated 5 June, 1676.—J. C. J.]

St. Christopher's, 22 June, 1676.

Deare Cousen,—I writ to you by the 'Jacob and Mary,' by which I give you an accompt that your goods are safe in a storehouse, and have received but little dammage, but the poverty of this island makes the markett bad, and requires time to vend commodities. But I shall act for you as if it were for myself; and I finde in this season, whiles the shippes are here, a glut of merchandize, which makes the sales more slow then I hope they will bee hereafter. I promessed to send you word what is most vendible in these parts. First I shall give you as good advise as I can concerning those thinges you deale in, as your chaires that doe not fold, your bed-ticks, searges of cloth colures, your striped curtains and vallances, your carpets of low prices. But too many of these thinges would soone cloy the country, because they are not but for the better sort. The most part here lye in hammakers, sit uppon benches, cloath themselves in camies or some finer linen, and never cover the table but at meales. For your buckrams, printed stuffs, white searges, hangings or cushions, I would counsel you never to send any more, till you heare I have sold these. The other commodities are sometimes asked after, which makes me think they will sell in tyme. . . . Ther is no commoditie better in these partes than Madera wines. They are soe generally and soe plentifully drunk; being the only strong drink that is naturall here, except brandy and rum, which are too hott. I have noe more to request of you at present, but that you would, if possible, procure me a carpenter and a mason. They would bee verry usefull to mee, now that I am about to setle my plantation myselfe. For I intende to turne planter, and to set up a suger worke, which will cost me some pence, but much the lesse if I could have such servants. . . .

I am, Sir,
Your most hearty loving kinsman and servant,
CHRISTOPHER JEAFFRESON.

Postscript.—There is a parcell of bookes in an olde trunk at your house, amongst which there is one in folio, called " Cooke upon Littleton." Pray send it mee, and some of the other little law bookes, as " The Compleat Sollicitor;" for every one is his owne lawyer in these partes.

LETTER IV.

To the Writer's father-in-law, Colonel George Gamiell, London.

[*Note.*—There is no need to give the opening passages of this letter, which relate to Mr. Worley's pecuniary embarrassments and miscarriage, and from their repetition of matters, set forth in the letter of the 5th instant to the same correspondent, seem to have been penned for the Colonel's information, *in case* that epistle should not have reached its destination. It is noteworthy that the English settlers in St. Kitts, at the time when their interest was suffering under great depression, could afford to pay yearly to their political agent (or as he would be now-a-days styled ' Commissioner') in London so large a sum, as "from two to three hundred pounds," *i.e.* some £1250 per annum, at the present value of our currency.—J. C. J.]

St. Christopher's Island, 22 June, 1676.

Honoured Sir,— . . . . . To undertake sugar-making, I have great convenience for a worke; and I intend, God willing, to try my fortune in planting canes, notwithstanding the great discouragement I meete with, upon the accompt of the French, who are twice as strong as wee. But the island being allowed by all that know it to be, without exception, the best in these partes, if under the power of one prince only, I have great confidence that our king will make such provisions for the defence of his interest here, that the French will never have cause to boast of such an advantage, as would bee the entire enjoyment of soe pleasant and fruitfull an island; which incourages me to goe on to improve my concerns, as well as I can.

Wee have news of the death of Lieutenant Graybridge, who went to receive the souldiers' pay; upon which the Governour was pleased to discourse to me something concerning Captain George, whom the island did employ to act for them at home, and allowed him two or three hundred pounds per annum; for which he did little; and when they ordered him to petition for a frigate or two, to be sent hither for the security of the islands and theire trade, without which the inhabitants cannot live, he sent them this answer,—that in tymes of peace they had noe occasion for such a security, and in tymes of warre his Majestie had soe much to doe with his shipps, that he could not spare one. Soe it is thought they have withdrawn theire allowance to Captain George. I took this occasion to insist upon the obligation they had to you for what you had done for the isle; and that none had ever acted more effectually for its good than you had done; and that, had you obteyned your last request that the people from Surinam might have been brought hither, there would have beene noe occasion of fearing the French, as it is this day. For it is miserable to see how the French insult vs, and how they must be humoured upon all accounts to maintaine a faire correspondence betweene vs. There is order for a fort to bee built; but the inhabitants are soe wretchedly poore, that it is feared they will not be able to goe through with the designe, without some supplies and assistance from England. . . . . . .

I rest, Sir, your most obedient son-in-law and faithful servant.

CHRISTOPHER JEAFFRESON.

LETTER V.

To a gentleman (probably the Secretary, or Aid-de-camp, of Sir William Stapleton, Captain-General of the Leeward Islands), who had written to Christopher Jeaffreson for goods required for Lady Stapleton.

[*Note.*—It should be observed, that the first lady of the Leeward Isles is expected to pay the price of a carpet and hangings for her reception rooms, in sugar.—J. C. J.]

St. Christopher's Island, 18 August, 1676.

Sir,—In order to the fulfilling of your request, I answered your courteous letter by the first opportunity; and now, though the dangers of this season doe deferre most from venturing their goods in theire shops often, much less from exposing them to the unconstant sea, yet as I would, at the command of Madam Stapleton, or to serve her or yourselfe, hazard myselfe much farther, soe am I now ready to obey her ladyshippe in what she requires, and have sent up the goods you writt for, vizt—four pieces of cotton hangings, with a large Smyrna carpett. I have not any curtaines or vallance, but what I feare are of too ordinary a sort for her ladyshipp's use; but I have sent a piece of printed stuffe, which is very convenient for hanging of roomes, or for making of curtaines and vallance (with a good fringe, if it can be found in these partes). The carpet, at the lowest, is at seventeene hundred of sugar, being large and fine. The hangings are at five thousand together; but, if parted, the small peeces at twelve hundred per peece, and the large one at two thousand. The peece of printed stuff is at fourty pounds of sugar, per yard, or at nine hundred the peece. Thus I have given you the particulars of the goods and their lowest prices ; desiring you to take care of them that, if Madam Stapleton dislikes them, what you cannot dispose of may bee preserved from the accidents of the season, for wett will bee verry apt to indommage them, especially the hangings ; and you will obleige extremely, Sir,

 Your most faithful friend and servant,
   CHRISTOPHER JEAFFRESON.

Postscript.—I pray you present my humble service to the Generall and his Lady.

LETTER VI.

To the Writer's cousin, John Jeaffreson, Esq,, of Roushall, Clopton, Suffolk.

[*Note.*— As the executor of his uncle, Colonel John Jeaffreson, the John Jeaffreson, to whom this letter is addressed, was plaintiff in the suit of " Jeaffreson, executor of Jeaffreson *against* Morton, Dawson and others, Tertenants of Yarway," (Easter, 21 of Carl. II. Roll. 291 or 201), reported in Saunders's Reports, *Vol. II. Part I.* The writer's remarks about the various plantations, which had belonged, or were believed to have belonged to his father in the island, are indicative of the confusion and defectiveness of the titles by which many of the earlier settlers in the West Indies held their land. In the omitted portions of this letter, minute but uninteresting particulars are given respecting the writer's proceedings against his bankrupt and fraudulent tenant, Mr. Worley.—J. C. J.]

St. Christopher's Island, 11 November, 1676.

Dear Cousen.— .... Now I must doe what I can, and I intend, God willing, to contynue some tyme here to settle my plantation, and build a sugar-worke; which will bee a great charge, but I esteeme it only as soe much ventured, as the merchants doe at sea. In the mean tyme I desire you would do me the favour to receive Mr. Marshland's rent, and retourne it to my brother Brett; for I shall be forced to draw some moneys or goods over hither towards the settlement of my plantation, for which, when it is settled, I hope I may find an honest and able tenant, or may place such an one upon it, as may make more considerable retournes into England, than have been ever yet made.

But I admire that I have never had nor seene any deed, by which my father held this manor of Wingfield, but only that from the Lord Carlisle, which nominates only a thousand acres. After he had made choice of which plantation, I suppose there was (or ought to have beene) some deed from the Lord Carlisle or Sir Thomas Warner, setting forth the bounds of the said plantations. For I finde the lease of Serjeant Delve bounding this manor, with the river to the east and Merrifield's Gutt to the west. Notwithstanding which, one Mr. Garbrants holdes a large slip of land, betweene mee and the gutt, which he had by marrying the daughter of one Mr. Partridge, to whom some say my father gave that plantation for his life, who is now dead. But Mr. Garbrants pretends to hold it by deed from the Earl of Carlisle. He likewise holdes the Red House Plantation, where Captain Samuel Jeaffreson lived, which his son, my cousen

Samuell (who is now at Antegoa, and whom I have never yet seene) solde to Delve who, when the island was lost, gave it to his goddaughter, the child of this Mr. Garbrants, a Dutchman. Mr. Garbrants saith that you satisfied Delve, when he was in England, that he might safely buy it. Upon which grounds he made up the bargain. Pray give me what instructions you can in these concerns in your next letter, as alsoe concerning a plantation which my father had on the wineward side of the island, called the Grange, which my cousin Robert Jeaffreson, as some say, solde to Mr. Watkins, and that the money was payd. Some call it mine. Soe many people are buzzing these things in my eares, I would gladly know as much as they; not that I have any intention of being troublesome. It is now in the hands of a Frenchman, one Mr. Helote (now in London) who married Mrs. Watkins, the brightest starr in our horizon. But chiefly I desier to be armed against the menaces of Lieutenant-Colonel Morton's friends; who declare that, after a long suite betweene his

father and mine, the business was referred
"home," and from thence hither, when coming
to a reference he recovered fourteen to sixteen
hundred thousand pounds of tobacco. This
Major Crook tould mee; and they pretend
that, if hee would renew the suite, hee might
have great advantages against mee, though I
know not in what. And yet wee are verry
good friends; but as I am forewarned, soe I
would be fore-armed. Mr. Worley hath
several writings that belong to mee, which
hee read at a reference; but he denies to
deliver them till I sue him for them; and
some, as I am informed, which concern
Colonel Morton, he hath delivered to some
of his friends, with an intent to prejudice
me, I having obtained a verdict against him
for the bare rent, to bee payed here without
interest or damages. He is a prisoner
between the two rivers, which you know
is a kind of King's Bench, which makes him
careless of paying his debt. There is one
Hemskerke, a Dutchman, that lives upon the
Godwin Plantation, and pays forty thousand
weight of sugar per annum for it and the

stock. I believe Captain Freeman will never recover his right in it, who, some say, bought it but for twelfe years of my father; but I can give no credits to any of these reports. . . . . . .

Your affectionate kinsman,
CHRISTOPHER JEAFFRESON.

CHAPTER III.

THE CONTINUATION OF THE FIRST YEAR
IN ST. CHRISTOPHER'S ISLAND.

(11 *November*, 1676, *to* 24 *May*, 1677).

Rival Colonies—Proposed Treaty of Neutrality—Current Values of Sugar and Indigo—Currency—Wages—Agriculture—English Military Force in St. Christopher's Island — French Predominance — Fight between the French and Dutch at Tobago—The Two Nations—Dutch Privateers—Destructiveness of War in the West Indies —Trade of St. Christopher's Island—Shipping at Nevis— Lockier's Pills.

LETTER VII.

To the Writer's cousin, Mr. William Poyntz, Upholder, at the sign of "the Goat," in Cornhill, near the Royal Exchange, London.

[*Note.*—The unpublished portions of this long letter give minute instructions respecting the size and quality of the copper still, three coppers, ladles, skimmers, cooler, scooper, and other implements and fittings, to be sent out from London for the writer's new sugar-works. Reference is made to the probability of war with France. Particulars are also given of certain barrels of indigo, consigned by the writer to Mr. Poyntz, who may be regarded as his West Indian cousin's London agent in commercial affairs. The statement of the current values of indigo and sugar will enable the reader to ascertain the value in money of commodities, sold for given quantities of those staples.—J. C. J.]

St. Christopher's, 14 November, 1676.

Dear Cousen.—I thanke you for your kinde letter. It was a cargo of loving expressions and came to no bad markett; but in a particular manner I acknowledge your courtesie in giving mee so early advice of those clouds that threaten us from the French horizon; though I hope they will all bee dispersed. But it may bee a great advantage to vs here, upon some accounts, if wee could be sure to have timely notice of an approaching war; for, as wee look upon it, the victory in these parts is gained more by strikeing the first blow, than by a multitude of blows. Wee had a rumour of the same before I received yours, but now that report is quelled; and wee now talk of a particular amity between vs and oure neighbours in this island, which has been formerly treated of and almost concluded:—that the French and wee should maintaine oure peace betweene ourselves, whatsoever happen betweene our princes at home. It would be the only way to make this island flourish, but I doubt it will never come to that. Which *if* it did, it would be worth while to send the commodities hither; whereas now the Frenche, who are richer by farre than wee, hardly dare trade with us, lest theire goods should be seized, nor dare the English trust them, who have not the liberty of bringing in theire sugar :—but that, indeed, is chiefly occasioned by the rigidness of theire West India Companie. . . . . . You forgot to give me advice what prices sugar and indigo bear at home. But I desier you would by your next tell me what the cleare profits of this 484 pounds eight ounces of indigo comes to in London; for it goes current here at two shillings the pound, that is, every ounce is worth a pound of sugar, which is valued here at three half-pence; sixteene pounds of sugar for one pound of indigo. . . . . . . Madera wine is now a drugg, by reason of a glut, which seldom happens. But it is no sure commodity.

LETTER VIII.

To the Writer's cousin, Mr. William Poyntz, Upholder, at the sign of "the Goat," in Cornhill, near the Royal Exchange, London,

[*Note.*—The letter opens with an acknowledgment of the arrival of goods, excellent in quality and condition, from London. From the particulars of the current rates of wages in St. Kitts, it appears that the skilled workman, bound to serve for four years, ordinarily received for his four years' service (in addition to board, lodging and clothes) four thousand pounds of sugar, worth twenty-five pounds sterling in Charles the Second's time, and some £125 at the present value of money. Ordinary servants received sugar to the value of only £1 17s 6d. equivalent to about £9 7s 6d of present money, for the same term of service. Captain Freeman's agreement to pay a skilled workman thirty pounds sterling at the end of four years' service was no great advance above these wages; as if he sickened from the climate, or any other cause, for more than a month (as a new settler would probably, if not certainly, sicken), he was to make good the time lost in illness by working for the same length of time beyond the stipulated four years. The cost of a workman's passage from England to the Leeward Isles (about five or six pounds) was paid by the employer engaging him in the mother-country.—J. C. J.|

St. Christopher's, 11 May, 1677.

Dear Cousen.— ..... I am, sorry I missed the workemen you write of. I was to blame for not giveing you more full instructions, which I hope will not bee altogether too late now. I confess all servants are very acceptable here; and if any laborious and industrious men would transporte themselves, I should gladly receive them and allow them the coustoms of the country, with meate, drinke, lodging and clothing, as are necessarie; but it is not the custome to promesse any more then three hundred pounds of sugar at the end of their term of four yeares. A great manie upon this account are carried every yeare to Jamaica and Antegoa. But for a good carpenter I would allow him foure thousand of sugar, or a little more, rather than faile, for his foure yeares service, and the like to a good cooper, and soe to a mason. For it is but just, such workemen should have some consideration for their tyme, more than others. But it is not the least of theire advantages, that, having all things provided for them while they are strangers, at the expiration of theire terme (which is vsually four yeares, sometymes three) they beeing well knowne at first setting up for themselves, theire gaynes are verry considerable; soe that they may soone grow riche, if they bee good husbandes. Whereas if they come out upon their owne accompt, they may chance to be fast in prison for debt, before it is knowne of what trades they are of. Captain Freeman hath sent over severall servantes and workemen, as a cooper or two, a carpenter, &c., as now lately he sent a young lusty carpenter, a sober man and good workeman, with his indentures to this effect :—that he should serve full foure yeares from the day of his arrivall at Nevis, and, if hindered from his worke by sicknesse or the like for above a month, he should make good the tyme over and above the foure years in which he was soe hindered; and for his trew and faithful service he was to receive thirty pounds sterling. His passage was payd at London, from whence he was consigned to Mr. Robert Helmes at Nevis, who shewed me the indenture. The thousand of sugar per annum usually sounds bigger in England the valew in cash . . . . . I have not kept a man in a storehouse for allmost these six monthes. The most vendible goods being disposed of, I found it not worth the while. Soe I brought them to my owne house; and at first neighbours were cautious of dealing with my man least I should bee too hasty and severe upon them, but now they are better satisfeyed. Merchandizing here is allmost as advantageous as planting, if a man have wherewithal to carry on a brisque trade. . . .

Your faithfull friend and servant

CHRISTOPHER JEAFFRESON.

LETTER IX.

To the Writer's father-in-law, Colonel George Gamiell, London.

[*Note.*—Acknowledging the Colonel's approval of the writer's proceedings against Mr. Worley, this letter contains much that is of no present interest, regarding the affairs and character of that person. The remainder of the epistle affords a remarkable view of certain aspects of life in the Leeward Isles.—J. C. J.]

St. Christopher's Island, 12 May, 1677.

Honoured Sir.—. . . . . I goe on expending money upon my plantation, in hopes it will repaye mee with interest; but I must have patience, for it will require tyme, as well as a large expense, before the sugar-worke can bee perfected. It is now esteemed here a great folly for a man to expose his tyme or goods to the hazard of indigo or tobacco, sugar being now the only thriveing and valuable commodity. I have had some offers for the renting of my land; but I have not thought them considerable, after soe much has beene layde out upon it, though I am something cautious of running too hastily into debt, considering our condition in this island, where we have scarce five hundred able English men, comprehending the two thin companies his Majestie is pleased to maintaine here. The French are three or foure tymes the number (if not more), though they lost two hundred of theire old soldiers and best men (if not more) with theire deputy-governour (under Monsieur D'Estrées) at Tobago; where, according to relation, there was the hottest service that many ages can tell of; it being very easie with the help of wind and current to enter the harbour, but very difficult to get out.

The Dutch lost ten or eleven of theire

ships; and the French six, that is to say, four great ships, a fire-ship, and a small vessell with a great number of theire men. Those that went on shoar were layd in ambuscade; but, beeing discovered by accident, the great shot from the Fort gave them a bloudy allarme. Those of this island behaved themselves gallantly, and were most of them layd in the bed of honour. The Count D'Estrées lost his ship, and was put to his shifts; and our governour Mathews's son, (a young lad of some fourteene yeares of age or thereabouts), who went volunteer, and was on board the same ship, escaped upon a piece of timber. The last day of Aprill, the Count D'Estrées arrived here, and delivered the young gentleman to his father, but intends he shall goe for France in the quality of an ensigne, in hope of greater preferment at the French court,—which our governour is not unwilling to consent to.

There is at present a very good understanding betweene the two Nations upon this island; and it hath beene (according to outward appearance) the desire of both parties to establish soe firme a league between vs, (and to get it ratified by the two kings) that whatsoever difference happen in Europe, a perpetual amity may bee retained and preserved here. But in the meane tyme, the French are erecting two Land fortes, contrary to what has beene formerly practised in this island. But 1 thinke they only took example by vs; who are indeavouring to raise such a fortification as may serve both for sea and land; but the great taxes, requisite to the carrying on soe great a worke, seems soe intollerable to the poore inhabitants, that severall leave the island. Insoemuch that, whilst wee acquire some strength by fortifycations, wee grow weake by depopulation; though the work bee very necessarie, in case of a suddaine rupture, for a retreat till some succours arrive from Nevis, upon which this island hath some dependence. But those hopes would be frustrated; if our Generall were not (as wee hope he will bee) furnished with a frigate or two upon such an occasion, for the transporteing of himselfe and men, who otherwise would run a great risque of beeing taken by any French man of warre or privateer, that may lye at Basse Terre.

Nor could this island well subsist in a tyme of warre, without two or three of his Majesties ships to secure the coast and trade; for it has beene found of late that both Dutch and French have made great preparations, and have carried on the warre very vigorously in these partes.

Some five days before Monsieur D'Estrées arrived here, one Sansbeck with six Dutch privateers came to an anchor here at Sandy Poynt, and are gone to Leeward. But he had not the courage to take three or foure ships out of the road of Basse Terre, because one was a man of warre; but she was disabled, having lost her maine-mast at Tobago; and most of her men, sick and wounded, were on shoar; and she rid a great way from the land. But theire designes are for plunder, where there is lesse danger. They report that eight or nine States' ships are arrived at Tobago, where a supply has beene long expected.

The wars here are more destructive then in any other partes of the world; for twenty yeares' peace will hardly resettle the devastation of one yeares' warre. As appeares by this island, where the sad workes of the last unhappy difference, in the yeare sixty-six, are not halfe worne out; nor is the island a querter so well peopled as it then was. Nor is there any great hope of the contrary; seeing soe few white servants are sent hither, and those that doe come are most of them Irish. Yet even in the poore condition this island is now in, it is farre more considerable to his Majestie, and the interest of England, than in former tymes, when it vas in the most flourishing condition, while the Hollanders managed the trade here, who kept theire storehouses mostly amongst the French, soe that the produce of the English plantations was carried either into the French groundes, or shipped for Holland, whilst theire commodities were vended here. 'Tis trew the planter found the sweet of this, for they sould cheape, and allowed a yeare or two for payment. But now the growth and goods of our owne nation are taken off by the inhabitants; and theire sugar or indigo &c., are shipt in English bottomes for Enggland, to the encrease of his Majesties customes, and the encouragement of navigation. And more, since the warres between Holland and France, the French are forced to deale with our merchants, insoemuch that a great part of their sugar is likewise shipped for England. I believe there are no lesse than forty or fifty saile of ships that come to this island and Nevis every year; but few of them to this island as yet, it being not so well setled. The most part of the goods are brought hither in shallopes, in which the sugars are returned to the ships. . . . . The third instant, Count D'Estrées sailed from hence, but left a compagnie of souldiers here, with orders that another compagnie should he put on shoar here, in lieu of those lost at Tobago. There are a great many French and Dutch inhabitants in the English ground. A Hamburger bought part of my plantation of Delve, and hath enjoyed it till now as his owne. But I obteyned a verdict against him for it, and am now in possession of it myselfe, and have planted part of it with sugar canes.

I rest, Sir, your obedient son,
CHRISTOPHER JEAFFRESON.

LETTER X.

To Mr. Percivall, the Writer's Attorney and Steward of his Manor of Dullingham, and other estate in Cambridgeshire. Dated from St. Christopher's Island, on 13 May, 1677.

The steward is enjoined to be punctual in holding courts at Dullingham, and instructed to pay all moneys, received by way of rents or fines to the writer's brother-in-law, Charles Brett Esq., of Channell Row, Westminster. The writer hopes that the tenants on the Dullingham estate will be made to pay their rents punctually, and sends his love to one of those tenants, " honest Mr. Fyson and his mother."

LETTER XI.

To the Writer's friend, Mr. Millett of London. Dated from St. Christopher's Island, 13 May, 1677.

Touching the writer's imperfectly successful endeavours to dispose of a large consignment of Lockier's Pills, which Mr. Millett sent out to St. Christopher's Island. The writer has found two agents, one in the west part, and another ("who will talk like a mountebank") in the east of the island, who will try to sell the pills, for the usual factorage; but it is to be feared that the commodity will hang on hand. "One Captain North, a trader to these parts, who was at Nevis about a monthe ago," the letter reports, "brought about fifty boxes, and was forced to leave some of them with a friend to put them off. He has been a noted man for bringing ofteu of these pills."

CHAPTER IV.

THE SECOND AND THIRD YEARS IN ST.
CHRISTOPHER'S ISLAND.

(24 May 1677 to 24 May 1679).

Edward Thorn in England—Apprehensions of War—West Indian Rumours of War between England and France—Panic in St. Christopher's Island—Colonists in Arms—Count d'Estrées and his Fleet—A Bucaneer Fleet of Thirty Sail—A Fleet of Merchantmen—The Alarm at Nevis—Withdrawal of the Fleets—A Suit in Chancery—Ventures in the West Indies—Success in Commerce—Expenditure on Planting—Goods sent out from England—A Salesman on Commission—Colonial Needs.

LETTER XII.

To the Writer's cousin, Mr. William Poyntz, Upholder, at the sign of "the Goat," in Cornhill, near the Royal Exchange, London. Dated from St. Christopher's Island, 22 June, 1677.

Instructing Mr. Poyntz to furnish Ensign Edward Thorn, the bearer of the letter, with £200 sterling, wherewith to pay for "a cargoe of goods fitt for this island," and begging Mr. Poyntz to assist in the selection and shipment of the same goods. "If," the writer continues, " you have any intentions of makeing a venture for these partes, he can informe you very well what commodities are most vendible here; but if there should bee a certainty of warre with the French, I would not hazard too much. Little more than the halfe will serve the turne; but I hope wee shall have peace. Then with the blessing of God I hope to recruit what I am now forced or invited to expende, and then, if I live, I may myselfe retourne to give you thanks for all your favours.

LETTER XIII.

To Mr. Helmes at Nevis, dated from St. Christopher's Island, 21 July, 1677.

Touching 7712 lbs. of sugar sent from the writer's new sugar works, per shallope, to the care of Mr. Helmes, for shipment at Nevis.

LETTER XIV.

To the Writer's father-in-law, Colonel George Gamiell, London.
St. Christopher's Island, 30 May, 1678.

Honoured Sir.—Had the divers reports and plausible rumours of a warre, already declared in Europe betweene his Majesty and the French king, beene backed with the certaine news of it, or had any orders for hostilities reached these islands before the 27th of April, I much doubt that the English interest upon this island would have been reduced to two acres of ground, which, as it had pleased God wee had indifferently well fortified it, wee resolved, by his assistance, to have defended if possible, till some succors arrived; assuring ourselves that the news of a warre would not much out-saile his Majesties fleete.

About the middle of February, we received the allarme, which made vs, considering the heaviness and chargeableness of our stone worke, resolve to carry on the rest of the work with earth and turfe, as it was at first intended. Only faggots were added for the support of the worke, and for expedition. Every weeke, a third part of the island, as well white men as negroes, came to assist.

The Count D'Estrées with his fleete was rideing then at anchor, at the island of Martinique. But our jealousies were much increased by the arrivall of a fleet of Bucaneeres, of about two thousand men, at this island, with the governour of St. Domingo, whence they were sent for by the Count D'Estrées. This only made vs more vigilant till the fifteenth of April, when the French governour sent our governour word by a person of note, that the warre was certainely declared in France, and that we might verry suddainely expect the arrivall of the fleete here.

Generall Stapleton, together with Colonell Mathews, his deputie here, having beene all along very diligent, omitting nothing that might tende to the security of his Majestie's interest or people, finding the vaste disproportion in number betweene vs and the enemy, the whole island were drawne into the forte—free men in armes, the slaves like pioneers. No man was idle. Every man bore a share of the labour. And it was admirable to see with what courage and resolution all our men quitted their habitations and interest, which they could not in reason hope to enjoy againe, till the enemy were reduced by a greater force. How well every man was fitted for the work. Not the least concerne appeared in their countenances.

The nineteenth day, the Count D'Estrées came with his fleet to an anchor in Basse Terre road, where he joyned with the bucaneere fleete, which made altogeather thirty odd sayle. By this tyme oure fort was in a very good condition for defence, thirty pieces of cannon being mounted in it, and seven hundred men, well armed and very well provided with victuals and ammunition. But wee found the Count D'Estrées waited for orders to fall on, and that the Count De Blanarque was provided with a power to make peace in these islands; upon which they made some overtures to our governour, who with the National commissioners gave a meeting to Mr. St Laurence and the French commissioners; but nothing was done in it. Then, the twenty-fifth, some ships, standing downe towards our fort, made vs stande to our armes, but they passed quietly by, being, as we afterwards heard, merchantmen only.

But, on the twenty-sixth, the whole fleet set sayle, and stood to windward, bearing in neare upon Nevis, where the allarme having beene given early in the morning, they were in an excellent posture to receive them, the Generall having for some time taken vp his quarters in the towne, still keeping the planters in armes. They were well inured to discipline and duty. There were six hundred horses ready to transport men speedily to those places where the enemy should give the attack, as it was expected he would; with several field-pieces in a moving posture. The ablest negroes, to the number of a thousand, were armed with speres; and the whole island was soe well fortified with trenches and small fortes, that they would have found hott service, had they attempted to land.

But they continued not much longer theire course to windeward, after having passed that island, before they tacked and stood to the southward. Upon what designe they are gone, wee are wholly ignorant. Only it is believed by most that they are gone to garrison. These coasts being thus cleared, our garrison was reduced againe to a third part of the island, till the two Generalls have agreed upon some articles of peace, to be observed amongst these islands (if theire Majesties thinke fitt), not much differing from what was formerly done by Sir Thomas Warner.

Your obedient sonne-in-law.
CHRISTOPHER JEAFFRESON.

LETTER XV.

From the Writer's brother-in-law, Charles Brett, Esq., of Channell Row, Westminster.

[*Note.*—Charles Brett, who married the letter-writer's only sister Mary, was the only son of Major-General Brett of Rotherby, Co. Leicester, at one time Governor of the Isle of Wight, by Frances daughter of Sir Henry Neville of Billingsbeere, Co. Berks, Kn^t., and widow of Sir Richard Worsley first baronet of Appuldercombe. A gentleman pensioner in ordinary at Whitehall, Charles Brett had for his first wife, Anne, daughter of Sir Ambrose Browne, first baronet of Beechworth Castle, Co. Surrey. His marriage with his second wife, Mary Jeaffreson, was solemnized in Westminster Abbey on 3 March, 167$\frac{2}{3}$, when she was twenty-three years of age. On his death in May, 1682, Charles Brett was interred in St Margaret's Church, Westminster, where his memorial tablet is preserved in one of the vestibules of the church. The letter-writer preserved to the last a strong affection for his brother-in-law, to whom he entrusted the chief control of his English affairs during his absence from England.—J. C. J.]

St. Christopher's Island, 31 May, 1678.

Dear Brother.—...... The advice of our overthrow in Chancery did not surprise mee soe much, as the contrary would have done; because this is but what I expected. Neither has it so discouraged mee, but that, if there bee any footsteps of justice left upon the earth, I should bee willing to trace them. I am glad Mr. Baker has beene soe long acquainted with the cause, as to be satisfied of the equity of it; and if he findes any other grounds (for I finde the justice of a cause to bee often tymes its greatest foe) to lay the foundation of our hopes upon, I desire that he would not give our enemie a tyme to breathe; or, if you perceive that there is any likelyhood or appearance of a recovery of that estate, or any part of it, I am clearly for another tryall; and for that end, I pray you present my service to Mr. Baker, and tell him, if he thinks fitt to revise the cause anew, I hope he will want noe iucouragement. Nor doe I desire he should spare anything, that shall bee necessary to put life into the businesse, whiche, if he retrieves it, shall bring him profitt as well as reputation in the end. It is not for vs mortalls to forejudge events. Wee must walke according to appearances, I hope Mr. Percivall will prove himselfe an honest man —I ever tooke him for such; but, as he is a man of generall businesse, it is necessary to reminde him of particulars by frequent calling upon him. Doubtless he will give a just account of the perquisites; for, when I come to look over the list of tenants, I should easily discerne if it were otherwise, for first the quit-rents are certaine (though not soe easily payd), and the fynes are upon the chainge of tenants, whether by succession, purchase, forfait or otherwise, according to the value of the estate. If Cousen Jeaffreson seems something peevish in his style, I hope your goodness will impute it to his age. I know my tenant Marshland to be a cunning fellow, and I always imagined that he wheedled the olde gentleman; but, if he has beene soe lavish upon repaires as my cousen writes (though I hope he mistakes, putting

pounds for shillings), if ever I live to see
him, I will bee satisfied that he had some
authority for soe doing, or else I shall very
unwillingly allow it. His being as it were
a neighbour of Cousen Jeaffreson, made me
desire him to look after that small estate,
rather than adde that to the other troubles I
give you, which are, indeed, of themselves
too many and too great.

    Your most faithful,
      CHRISTOPHER JEAFFRESON.

LETTER XVI.

To the Writer's cousin, Mr. William Poyntz, Upholder, at the sign of "the Goat," in Cornhill, near the Royal Exchange, London.

    St. Christopher's Island, 31 May, 1678.

Dear Cousen.—I received yours of the
22nd of January by Edward Thorn, who
happened to arrive in a very troublesome
tyme, when there was noe other businesse
to bee done, but what related to armes and
warre, which last was sayd to bee all ready
declared in Europe ; which made me resolve
with him to putt our goods on shoar at

Nevis, where, since our troubles are blown over, I thinke he hath mett with noe bad markett. I have not yett seene his account of sales, but you shall heare more particularly of those affairs by the next opportunity. I pray, God blesse your babes, my little cousens, and increase their stock. I shall use my diligence for your sake and theirs in taking care of what you have sent. I hope you will not take it amisse, that I drew soe considerable a summe out of your hands at once. I endeavoured by tymely notice to prepare you for it beforehand. As I am here in a remote islande, I would willingly make some use of my tyme by improveing my stock as well as I can, which, if it were much larger than it is, I could better menage than now I doe, inasmuch as it would be more worth my tyme. I thanke God, hitherto the goods, I have received, have more than answered my expectations; but all has been flung like seede into my plantation, in which I have had a very considerable losse by those troubles,—more then I will speak, seeing that if they terminate here I shall have no

cause to complaine. But why doe I say
'complaine?'—seeing that in all conditions
we are to blesse God without murmuring.

I rest, Your trewly affectionate Cousen,

CHRISTOPHER JEAFFRESON.

[Immediately after this letter there is
entered into the Letter-Book a Memorandum
of the articles for a Treaty of Neutrality,
between the British Colonists under the
governorship of the Captain-General of the
Leeward Islands, and the French Colonists
under the government of the French king's
Lieutenant-General by sea and land in
America, agreed upon and settled in the
year 1678 by commissioners appointed for
that purpose; with copies of documents relating to the same futile convention.—J.C.J.]

LETTER XVII.

To the Writer's cousin, Mr. William Poyntz, Upholder, at the sign of "the Goat," in Cornhill, near the Royal Exchange, London.

[*Note.*—The unpublished parts of this
prolix letter, relate to the satisfactory sale,
by Mr. Edward Thorn, at Nevis, of the

goods landed there at the commencement of the late preparations for war. Having shown his confidence in this smart young man by sending him to England to purchase goods to a large amount, the writer declares his undiminished regard for a person, who, in the course of a few years, became his treacherous and fraudulent steward.—J.C.J.]

St. Christopher's Island, 23 July, 1678.

Dear Cousen.— ...... I should bee sorry that you should finde him (*i.e.*, Edward Thorn) any other then I esteeme him to bee, that is a very just, honest fellow. If he proves otherwise, we may both be losers. Yet I have confidence in him. I would entrust him with all I am worth in these parts; and it is a small commendation to my neighbours here that I know not one man more in the Indies I would do the like to, unlesse upon necessity, because I have not had the same experience of them, and am too apt to bee afrayd of my friends. I now begin to draw my businesse to a head, and may very shortly expect some retournes for all my trouble and expence, which were never greater than at present. The many pull-backs and hindrances I have mett with here putt me behindhand, soe that I must look homeward for a supply. In order whereunto I have desired my brother to fournish you with one hundred pounds or thereabouts to lay out on such things as I have named in the enclosed note, which I have calculated will, with the charges of freight and customes, come within the aforementioned sum. But in that I may be mistaken. I trust wholy to your judgement, which I have always found very good. Only as to those that concerne my owne weareing apparrell, especially the ribbonds and cravat, I would bee assisted by the fancy of my sister, which I allways approved very good.

   Your affectionate Cousen,
    CHRISTOPHER JEAFFRESON.

THE ENCLOSED NOTE.

Two and a quarter yardes of broad cloath of about 17s. per yard.

Silke suitable and fashionable for lineing.

One paire of silke stockins, suitable with sowing and stiching silke.

Ribbonds to make a fashionable trimeing and to tye the sleeves.

Three castors from 15s. to 20s. price, and two castors from 12s. to 15s.

6 felts of 3s. or 4s. or 2s. 6d. price per hatt.

One lace cravatt and cuffs genteele, but not too riche.

Two dozen of plaine shoes.

15 yardes of slight greene searge for livery.

20 yardes of worsted livery lace, mixed greene, redde and white.

20 yardes of a deepe red tammy, and 15 yardes of yellow tammy.

Two dozen pounds of browne thread.

Fourty ells of Holland, 15 ells at 2s. 6d. p. elle; 15 ells at 3s. 6d. p. elle; and 10 ells at 4s. p. ell.

200 yardes of blew lining.

4 peeces of Kenting; two of 8s. p. peece, and two of 12s. p. peece.

200 ells of canvas; 150 yardes of browne ossenburgs.

100 yardes of white ossenburgs.

52 ells of broad Dowles.

15 yardes of sad cullered Irish freeze of an ordinary sort.

Three peeces of sad cullered mixt searges of 25s. p. peece.

8 yardes of persian taffety suitable for lineing.

Two peeces of sad cullered mixt searges at about 26s. p. peece.

15 yardes speckled Callico suitable.

4 grosse of silver, and 5 gross of silke coat-buttons suitable.

20 yardes of white fustian about 8d. per yard.

30 yardes of German linen about 1s. 6d. per peece.

14 pounds of whited brown thread; half a pound of fine.

100 lb. of Castill soape or Aleppo soape; or half one, half the other, if the commodety be deare.

100 lb. weight of harde well-made candles.

4 dozen of knives of 3d. 4d. 5d. and 6d. prices.

One pound of thread of all colours.

A short cane; and two or three oaken sticks with heads.

LETTER XVIII.

To the Writer's cousin, Mr. William Poyntz, Upholder, at the sign of "the Goat" in Cornhill, near the Royal Exchange, London. Dated from St. Christopher's Island, 3 May, 1679.

Having given several reasons for fearing that he will not be able to sell Mr. Avery's goods to a great profit, the writer continues, "I am afraid the couch and the printed stuffs will never clear the prime costs. For the first, a merchand at Nevis, that hath had one these two yeares, could never sell it; and for the latter, you know the printed stuffs you ventured with, wee never sold here at all, only one blew peece, which I meerly persuaded one to take as fashionable, and am not yet paid for it, (but it is a good debt). For the other stuffs, they shall vend according as people fancy. The butter, cheese and candles are usually very good commodities, but I never knew them and all other provisions soe cheape as now."

CHAPTER V.

THE FOURTH YEAR IN ST. CHRISTOPHER'S ISLAND.

(24 May, 1679, to 24 May, 1680).

Colonial Agents in London—The English Colonists of St. Kitts require a new London Agent—The Agency offered to Colonel Gamiell—French Insolence and Discourtesy—Assassination of an English Soldier—Slaves landed at Nevis—A great Fire at Boston—Commercial Dullness in New England—William Calhoun—Colonel Matthews—Sir William Stapleton and the Count de Blanarque—Futile Negotiations for an Anglo-French Treaty of Neutrality—The Gallants of the Leeward Islands—Ventures in New England.

LETTER XIX.

To the Writer's father-in-law, Colonel George Gamiell, London.

[*Note.*—This letter is noteworthy, as it relates to the duties of a Political Agent (or 'Commissioner,' as he would now-a-days be called) for a West Indian Colony, and shows the mode of his appointment. The writer was by this time a Member of the Assembly, and was taking an active part in negotiations for the proposed Anglo-French Treaty of Neutrality in the West Indies.—J.C.J.]

St. Christopher's Island, 10 July, 1679.

Honoured Sir.—Since the receipt of your last letter, bearing date the 22nd of November, I have writt several letters, which I hope are come to your handes, but could not answer it fully, as I could have wished. Since which, there hath happened something in relation to what you there mention, where, though you are pleased to excuse your not interesting yourselfe in the publick affaires of this island, I am not ignorant of the obligations wee have to you for the assistance you gave our agent in that verey matter he was employed in. And indeede (as I could doe no lesse), I have beene allways forward (where that discourse has beene suitable) to put the planters in minde, to whom wee owe many priviledges wee now enjoy. I finde some of them very sensible of it, as they are of the advantages that might accrew to our island, by having an agent in London, to promote its interests there. But the bad successes they have had in the persons formerly employed, have soe far discouraged them, that they have not willingly embraced any proposition of that nature; till yesterday, that at a meeting of the Governor, Councill and Assembly, it was considered how necessary it is that the affaires of this island should be put into the hands of some particular friende at home. The difficulty in findeing out a fit person, in whom they might put confidence, that he would really and faithfully act for vs on all occasions, was the only obstacle to the matter, which was soon removed by the mention of your name, whose worth and honor are not unknown to some in these partes; and whose constant good inclinations towards this island, and many good offices formerly done by you in its behalf, were sufficient encouragement to them, to pitch upon you as the most fitt person, to be soe intrusted, if you would be pleased to accept of the offer, and to take the trouble upon you. But as nothing of this nature is to be done without the consent of our General, the Assembly have requested our governour (who goes up to Nevis to-morrow) to propose the businesse to his Excellency :—that he would give vs leave to employ a friend to take care of the affaires of this island in particular. Which if he consents to, you will receive shortly some proposalls from our Governour, &c., touching this matter. The Assembly seemes willing to give £100 sterling per annum gratuity, if you thinke fitt to espouse the country's interest. Thus much I thought good to acquaint you with; for the present hopeing to give you a further accompt by Col. Hare, how General Stapleton rellishes the designe. I knowe he has a great kindness for Captain Freeman: but our islanders are not so fond of him. Be pleased not to take notice to any body, that I have given you this advice of our intentions beforehand, lest the General should oppose them. We have small hopes that the Articles of Peace agreed on should be

confirmed by the two kings; which makes
vs more jealous as to the designes of the
Count D'Estrées, who is lately arrived with
a squadron of seven capital ships in these
partes. They are gone to winter—that is,
till the hurricane season be past, or it may
be to bring the bucaniers againe, if a
rupture should happen (as has beene long
doubted betweene the two crownes). Wee
cannot immagine what soe many men of
warre should doe herein at a tyme of peace,
and they give it out that they expect more.
Theire ships are very unwilling to salute
his majesties forts. Two of them not long
since fired seven shot ashoar at Nevis, in
answer to some that were fired at them from
the fort, only to make them strike.

Your obedient sonne-in-law,
CHRISTOPHER JEAFFRESON.

LETTER XX.

To the Writer's father-in-law, Colonel Gamiell, London,
Dated from St. Christopher's Island, 9 September, 1679.

Announcing that, though he at first discountenanced the project, General Stapleton has consented to a second petition (presented to his Excellency by the letter-writer's own hand), that the planters of St. Kitts may retain the Colonel as their London Agent. Concerning the demeanour of the French islanders, the letter gives alarming intelligence. Their insolence increases. They daily break the articles of "the antient concord agreed on, at the first setlement and division of the island betweene the two nations, which in tyme of peace have ever since beene punctually maintained by both." They have even presumed to deny the English right of way through "the common pathes." An English soldier, in passing through their quarters by one of the said paths, has been assassinated, with "forty-two cuts and stabbs in his body." No English merchandise is allowed to enter the French quarter. Though their ships continue to ride in the English roads, the French will not permit English vessels to anchor in their waters. They recently committed a flagrant act of piracy in seizing and condemning as a prize, on a mere pretext, a slave-ship from the Guinea Coast that had just landed most of its negroes at Nevis. By the death of Colonel Stapleton (His Excellency's brother) Mountserrat, as well as Antigua, is without a governor.

LETTER XXI.

To the Writer's father-in-law, Colonel Gamiell, London. Dated from St. Christopher's Island, 17 November, 1679.

Enclosing a letter from the Council and Assembly of the island, inviting the Colonel to be the Political Agent in London.

LETTER XXII.

To the Writer's cousin, Mr. William Poyntz, at the sign of "the Goat," in Cornhill, near the Royal Exchange, London. Dated from St. Christopher's Island, 3 January, 16$\frac{79}{80}$.

Trade is unusually dull in the island; the depression being consequent on the badness of the sugar harvest,—the sugar plantations having been greatly injured by the alarm of war, which withdrew the workmen from the canes at a critical season. The writer's loss in sugar from that "all-arme" will be at least £200 sterling. Few merchant-ships have come out from Old England; the same being the case with New England. "But the New England men, who vsed to be the first at the markett, have probably beene kept back by the unfortunate fyer which happened this summer in Boston, and haith much distracted the merchants, and put them out of their ways." The active and enterprising Mr. Edward Thorn, in whose honesty the writer still puts perfect confidence, is in New England, on his employer's commercial business. In the meantime, the writer's particular friend, "Mr. William Calhoun, a Scotch merchant" who "haith dwelt upon this island ever since I knew it, and hath used the trade of these islandes these many yeares, and that to noe small advantage," is on his way to England, with a bill of exchange, payable a month after sight, drawn by the writer on his corespondent, who is instructed to honour the bill, and to offer Mr. Calhoun all the attentions due to his conspicuous merits.

LETTER XXIII.

To the Writer's father-in-law, Colonel George Gamiell, London.

St. Christopher's Island, 7 January, 16$\frac{78}{79}$.

[*Note.*—The two generals of this letter are General Sir William Stapleton, Bart., the English Captain-General of the Leeward Isles, and the Count de Blanarque, Governor and Lieutenant-General of His most Christain Majesty the King of France both by sea and land in America. J. C. J.]

Honoured Sir.—Myne of the seventeenth of November last, with the inclosed from the Council and Assembly of this island, I hope is come to your handes; but least they should be miscarried (beeing sent by way of Bristoll), I have taken this better opportunity to present you with the duplicate of the sayd letter and papers from the Council and Assembly, whiche are by the hands of one Mr. William Calhoun a merchant (a correspondent of Captain Crispes). A more intelligent person and more knowing of the state and interests of this and the neighbour islandes could not be found; for he hath used this trade, and dwelt upon this island, these many yeares, and hath beene elected as one of the representatives or Assemblymen thereof. He hath promessed me to deliver this to you with his own handes, which I was the more desirous to obleige him to, in regarde of the satisfaction which you may receive from him, better than by letters, if you should have an inclination to trouble yourself with the concernes of this island, or the knowledge of what is most wanting to be done or procured for its good. Colonel Matthews, our governour, was hindred from writing to you, according to his intentions by the last opportunity, by reason that the two generalls were then there. For an account of whose proceedings, and the quite contrary effects of them to what was hoped by both nations, I referre you to the bearer hereof, who was with me, when the Count De Blanarque broke off the treaty by refusing to signe the articles which I brought him, and which they had been so long agreeing upon; which was the last message that past betweene the two Generalls upon this island. But, as I said before, there is nothing of news, or that concernes these partes, which you may not better learne from Mr. Calhoun, than from my pen. Therefore with the tender of my most humble duty to you,

I rest, Sir, your obedient son-in-law,
CHRISTOPHER JEAFFRESON.

LETTER XXIV.

To the Writer's sister, Madam Brett, Channell Row, Westminster.

St. Christopher's Island, 7 January, 16$\frac{7 8}{7 9}$.

Deare Sister.—I have sought allmost impatiently for an opportunety to wishe you a merry New Yeare, and could find none till now (which is, as one may say, a day after the faire), by a bonny Scot who, contrary to the custome of his countrymen, is goeing home againe, and intends to stay some tyme in London by the way; where I have obleiged him to see some of my friends, and to deliver my letters. I must begge the favour of you so soone as you have leasure to buy me all necessaries for another suit of cloathes; that is, a hatt, a cravatt, and cuffs, one payer of silke and three payer of thread stockings, for my own wear, besides the cloath lining and all other materials for the suit; which I hope I may have before next Christmasse (which is almost a twelvemonth), if Cousin Poyntz does not let slip the occasions, as (under the rose) he has done many times of late. That is the reason I have not had above two letters from you these 13 or 14 months, which came within a month or two one of an other. But if I give you this trouble, blame not me, but your owne late ingenuous proceeding in the like afaire. I feare this suit will not last me tll I goe for England; if it doe, it will be no bsse. I praye, send me an embroidered or fashionble waist-belt, and let everything be modest and creditable; for the better sort in these islandes are great gallants, sometymes beyond their abilities, or at least their qualities. Pardon the freedom I take, and accept the tender of my hearty love and service, who am, your loving brother,

CHRISTOPHER JEAFFRESON.

LETTER XXV.

To the Writer's brother-in-law, Charles Brett, Esq., Channell Row, Westminster. Dated from St. Christopher's Island, 9 January, 16$\frac{79}{80}$.

Mr. Brett is entreated to furnish the writer's cousin, Poyntz, with £50 to meet the bill of exchange in Mr. Calhoun's hands. The writer assumes that Mr. Brett's receipts from the steward at Dullingham will enable him to do so without difficulty. Remembrances are sent to Sir Edward Brett and other friends.

LETTER XXVI.

To the Writer's cousin, Mr. William Poyntz, Upholder, at the sign of "the Goat," in Cornhill, near the Royal Exchange, London. Dated from St. Christopher's Island, 23 March, 1680.

The writer has not heard from Mr. Edward Thorn, since his arrival in New England, but expects to see the young man daily. He has sent to New England some of Mr. Avery's goods, " as being alltogether improper for these islandes and not vendible." The letter adds, " I have sent my sister a small casque of tamarines, marked 'B. No. 1.' which I desire you would see the delivery of."

LETTER XXVII.

To Mr. Timothy Clarke, merchant of Boston, but now of Nevis. Dated from St. Christopher's Island, 31 March, 1680.

Mr. Clarke is informed that Mr. Edward Thorn went to New England last October, with instructions and money to pay his account, together " with the £500 for the seamen." Possibly Mr. Thorn has done so, since Mr. Clarke's departure from Boston. The writer adds. "If I knew the price of your porke, I might deale with you for some, therefore I should gladly hear."

CHAPTER VI.

THE FIFTH YEAR IN ST. CHRISTOPHER'S ISLAND.

(24 May, 1680, to 24 May, 1681.)

Intrigues for the Agency—The Writer in Trouble—Edward Thorn's Absence and Reappearance—Scarcity of Artisans and White Labourers—Prospects of Emigrants—West-Indian Adventurers—The Writer in Love—Mistress Frances Russell's Age and Fortune – A Christening at Government House, Nevis—Death of Colonel Matthews—The Writer's Perplexities—His Resolve to spend another Year in the West Indies—Affairs at Dullingham.

LETTER XXVIII.

To the Writer's father-in-law, Colonel George Gamiell, London. Dated from St. Christopher's Island, 24 July, 1680.

TOUCHING the influences, which have inspired General Sir William Stapleton with unfriendliness towards the Colonel who, in consideration of the Captain-General's feelings, is disposed to give up the thought of becoming the island's Political Agent in London. "I could wish," says the writer, "I had beene only passive in the proposals made to you by this island, seeing the event is like to prove soe contrary to my hopes and expectations; which proceedes originally from the illoffices done you by somebody, who is so jealous of the interest he has in the General, that he is ready to fling dirt upon such as are like to overtake him in the advantages of these American employments. Whoever he is, he has noe kindness for St. Christopher's and less for yourselfe, as appeares by those impressions made in Sir William Stapleton's opinion concerning you, whom he has represented as an enemie to his interest."

LETTER XXIX.

To the Writer's cousin, Mr. William Poyntz, Upholder, at the sign of "the Goat," in Cornhill, near the Royal Exchange, London. Dated St. Christopher's Island. 3 August, 1680.

Condoling with Mr. Poyntz on the loss of his wife, and reporting that the writer has endured several disappointments and much sickness. "I should be tedious to you," says the writer, "should I enumerate the multitude of misfortunes and crosses, which have attended me these two or three yeares last past, and especially this last yeare, in which it hathe pleased God to visit not only myselfe but most of my family with sicknesse. But of His mercy He hath restored vs all to our healthes againe, excepting a few of my negro slaves, some of whom death hath freed from their bondage. These afflictions are bitter in the mouth, but sweete when digested. These bitter potions, which the heavenly physician seeth necessary for the soul, ought to be received with thanksgiving, not with murmurings." In no thankful strain, the writer goes on to state his anxieties respecting Mr. Edward Thorn, who went to New England in October last, on a commercial mission, in a vessel freighted with goods pertaining to his employer. Since Christmas, when the agent sent his master a letter from "Road Island," the writer has received no communication from the young man, whose prolonged absence and silence occasion his patron painful mistrust and apprehensions. The writer suspects, that after all his goodness to him, the active young man will prove an ungrateful and treacherous servant.

The remainder of letter (penned at two later dates, viz., 13 August, and 6 September) is in a happier vein. After passing through divers misadventures, and narrowly escaping shipwreck, Mr. Edward Thorn has reappeared under circumstances which prove him to be an honest and clever supercargo. The thirteen horses and mares, that he has brought from New England, have turned out a fortunate venture, though the animals suffered much on ship-board. One of them died; but the other twelve have been sold at high prices. Edward Thorn's master ends his letter in high spirits.

LETTER XXX.

To the Writer's cousin, Mr. William Poyntz, Upholder, at the sign of "the Goat," in Cornhill, near the Royal Exchange, London.

[*Note.*—The omitted portions of this letter relate to consignments of sugar and other merchandise made by the writer to his correspondent. The printed part affords a view of the condition of white labourers in our West Indian settlements, and points in a suggestive manner to the sources from which those colonies drew the larger part of their European population.—J. C. J.]

St. Christopher's Island, 6 May 1681.

Dear Cousen.— .... It is long since my request to you to sende me some white servants, especially a mason, carpenter, taylor, smith, cooper, or any handy craftsman; and now I am necessitated to reiterate my sayd request to you, not only for a clerke or tradesman, but for any sorte of men, and one or two women if they can be found. They are generally wanted in this island; and all my bond-servants are gone free. The last of them was Joseph Demure, formerly one of the porter's men belonging to the lodge at Whitehall. He is married and lives very well; though his father imagines him dead and writ to me for his wages, which I have payd him to the value of neare forty pounds sterling. Yet I was no loser by him, for he is a taylor and a good workman. I question not but that, if I were in London, I could take my choice. I remember the objection you retourned, in answer to my sayd request, was that people would make theire conditions before they would transport themselves. Which I acknowledged to be prudence in them. But usually such persons, as are volunteers for the West Indies, are under such circumstances, as may reasonably induce them to oblige themselves to an apprenticeship, at least for four yeares, in hopes of the advantages they may probably make for themselves at the ende of the terme, during which they are instructed in the nature and customes of the place.

It is seldome seene that the ingenious or industrious men fail of raising their fortunes in any part of the Indies, especially here, or where the land is not thoroughly settled. There are now several examples of it to my knowledge—men raised from little or nothing to vast estates. And I can assure you our slaves live as well now as the servants did formerly. The white servants are so respected that, if they will not be too refractory, they may live much better than thousands of the poor people in England, during their very servitude, or at least as well.

For a taylor, a cooper, a carpenter, a joyner, a mason, a smith,—which are the trades most necessary here,—I would allow to such an one, when a good workman, a thousand pounds of sugar wages, for each yeare that he should serve me, with what must be paid for theire passages, tools or instruments. For one that can handle his pen,—he may deserve as much, but wee seldome give it, because such men are more plenty, and have other advantages. As for labourers and menial servants, theire passages being payd, they must expect only food, raiment and lodgeing, until theire terme (which is never less than foure yeares) be expired, and then by the laws and customes of the island they are to have four hundred pounds of sugar, to begin the world with. Thus I have told you the conditions I would willingly make. But I do not tye you vp just to what I have proposed. A little more may be added, as you see convenient, and as much less as you please. Only the four hundred pounds of sugar will admit of noe abatement. For if Newgate and Bridewell should spew out their spawne into these islandes, it would meete with no lesse incouragement; for no goale-bird can be so incorrigible, but there is hope of his conformity here, as well as of his preferment, which some have happily experimented; insoemuch that all scrts of men are welcome to the publick, as well as the private interests of the island. Therefore, if you could sende me some of any sort of the aforementioned people, you would do me a singular kindnesse; and though I were intended for England, they would meete with good entertainement by those I should leave behinde me; for which purpose I have covenanted with Edward Thorn for a certain tyme, in case I had left the island, of which I am not at all resolved for the present.

Scotchmen and Welchmen we esteeme the best servants; and the Irish the worst, many of them being even good for nothing but mischief. I believe, if you will endeavour it, you may find Scotch and English, that would willingly change their clymate upon the aforementioned termes, and much more when they are directed to a certaine place and person, of whose character they may be well informed. How many broken traders, miserable debtors, penniless spendthrifts, discontented persons, travelling heads and scatter-brains would joyfully embrace such offers!—the first, to shun their greedy creditors and loathsome goales; . . . . . ; the third, to fill their bellies though with the bread of affliction; the fourth, to leave an unkinde mistresse or dishonest wife, or something worse; the fifth, to satisfie fond curiosity; sixth, he knows not why, unless to cross his friends, and seek his fortune. These and the like humours first peopled the Indies, and made them a kinde of Bedlam for a short tyme. But from such brain-sick humours have come many solid and sober men, as these modern tymes testify. . . . . . .

Dear Cousen &c., &c.,

CHRISTOPHER JEAFFRESON.

LETTER XXXI.

To the Writer's sister, Madam Brett, of Channell Row, Westminster. Dated from St. Christopher's Island, 5 May, 1681.

After announcing in diffuse language the death of Colonel Matthews, governor of the island, with whom he had intended to return to England, and the change which that event made in his plans and inclinations, the writer reveals his prudent passion for a young lady of adequate fortune and a strong connection in the Leeward Islands. " Seeing the small discourse," he remarks, " that was whispered abroad concerning Madam Russell, the governor of Nevis, his widow and myselfe, came to your hearing in so short a tyme, certainely this, which hath beene much more bruited, and with more reason, (concerning myselfe and Madam Francis Russell, daughter to the sayd Governour), cannot be hid from your knowledge. Nor is it my desire it should be. The gentlewoman is very young ; *fifteene* yeares of age, and *soe many* hundred pounds is the some of her portion, to be paid by her brother Sir James Russell at sixteene yeares of age, or day of marriage, besides four negroes. It was discoursed of as a suitable match some moneths before I saw her; and I heard of it some moneths before I saw her; and yet I continued my intentions of seeing you this spring, till the death of the Governour loosed me from the obligation of accompanying him. I began then to be on a balance in my reasons for goeing or staying, and I have multiplied arguments on both sides to a great number, and I continue doubtful whether to embrace the offer. I pray God direct me for the best. Mr. Thomson hath taken vp his abode with Captain Freeman of Antegoa (who married our cousen Robert Jeaffreson's widow). I saw him at Nevis, and proffered my service to him. I shall long to heare your sentiment of what I have informed you of. Possibly you may have seen the young gentlewoman with her sister, the Lady Stapleton, who brought her out of England, along with her. I shall not omit informing you upon all occasions of my proceedings in this affaire. In order to which I am suddainly bound vp for Nevis to the christening of Sir James Russell's daughter, where Colonel Cottar and I are to be godfathers, and the young lady one of the godmothers. . . . . . &c., &c.,

Your affectionate brother,

CHRISTOPHER JEAFFRESON.

LETTER XXXII.

To the Writer's brother-in-law, Charles Brett, Esq., of Channell Row, Westminster. Dated from St. Christopher's Island, 6 May, 1681.

Touching lightly on the writer's intentions towards Madam Francis Russell, and entering more fully into questions of business at Dullingham. Lord George —— must either renew his lease, or give up a holding on the writer's estate. The time is at hand, when terms must be settled for a removal of Mr. Fyson's lease. The writer is longing to see

England again. "When I left England," he says, "I did not resolve upon any stay, nor did I ever propose to myselfe a longer tyme than four yeares, which I thought a long tyme to be in the West Indies."

LETTER XXXIII.

To the Writer's father-in-law, Colonel George Gamiell, Dated from St. Christopher's Island, 6 May, 1681.

Informing the colonel of the writer's purpose to make Madam Francis Russell an offer. "I have," says the writer, "had some advice some moneths since, and lately fresh incouragements to make my addresses to Mrs. Francis Russell, own sister to the General's lady, with whom she hath her abode. Her fortune is better than fifteene hundred pounds sterling. Her age is but fifteene yeares; but the natives of these islands (and she is one) usually marry about that age. But I have not yet proposed the matter to herselfe, nor her neare relations; having been resolved to wave it; had not the death of Colonel Matthews put a suddaine check to my proceedings upon my voyage for England, which I meane now to suspend for this yeare in order to the amour I am entering upon, if I meete not with something to chainge my purpose."

LETTER XXXIV.

To the Writer's cousin, Mr. William Poyntz, at the sign of "the Goat," in Cornhill, near the Royal Exchange. Dated from St. Christopher's Island, 5 May, 1681.

Attributing his recent silence to his confident hope of seeing Mr. Poyntz in London, "this summer," the writer hints at the new interest which bids faire to detaine him in the Leeward islands for another yeare. " I see little hopes," he says, " of getting so soone clear of the West Indies; beeing now in some likelihood to enter into new bonds, such as may tye me by the legge for a tyme, and just in a manner as I was setting saile and putting off from these shoars, so neare was I to entering upon my voyage that ten days more had certainly put a period to my present being upon this island, had I not been interrupted in my designe by the death of the Governour, in company of whom I intended to take my passage. I am conscious that my silence hath been the occasion that the date of your last letter is very neare a twelvemonth olde." Mr. Poyntz is thanked for the care he takes of the writer's small interest at Walton.

LETTER XXXV.

To the Writer's maternal aunt, Madam Peacock, at Dullingham House, Cambridgeshire. Dated from St. Christopher's Island, 5 May, 1681.

Condoling with her on the recent death of "cousin Barber," and sending his "humble services" to Aunt Dayrell of Shudy Camps, Cambridgeshire.

LETTER XXXVI.

To Mr. Percivall, the Writer's steward and attorney in Cambridgeshire. Dated from St. Christopher's Island, 6 May, 1681.

Mr. Percival is entreated to give the writer's brother-in-law, Mr. Brett, full and regular information respecting affairs at Dullingham. He may not suffer Mr. Fyson " to be so much behind with his rent;" he should lose no time in arranging about the renewal of " Lord George's lease;" and " it would not be amisse" for him " to enquire after the two lives upon which the fellows of Clare Hall hold theire land." The writer observes also, " I am not well resolved whether you are constant in keepeing the Courts, especially the Court Leet once every year."

CHAPTER VII.

THE SIXTH AND LAST YEAR IN ST. CRISTOPHER'S ISLAND.

(24 May, 1681, to 24 May, 1682). *

Brave Clothing—Rejected Addresses—A strenuous Suit and baffled Suitor—Hurricanes in St. Christopher's Island —Injuries done to the Writer's House and Plantations— Sufferings inflicted by the Storms on the Writer's Slaves —His Exertions in their Behalf—Horses imported from New England—Aunt Peacock's Curiosity touching Mistress Frances Russell—Charles Brett's Good Services.

LETTER XXXVII.

To the Writer's cousin, Mr. William Poyntz, Upholder, at the sign of "the Goat" in Cornhill, near the Royal Exchange.

St. Christopher's Island, 25 July, 1681.

Dear Cousen.—Haveing writt to you

---

* The Writer spent in all six years and seven weeks in the Island; going on board the good ship 'St. Nicholas' for his homeward voyage on 12 July, 1682.

very lately, that is about twelve dayes since, by Captain Norwood, I have little to offer to you at present, but my hearty love and services. Only being likely to keepe my Christmasse here, I have desired you to take the trouble of sending me those necessaries hereafter mentioned, and I have desired my sister to assist you in the buying them (for fashion's sake); the modes being best known at the end of the towne where she lives. I had made provision of four or five hogsheads of sugar for this purpose; but for want of freight according to my desire, I ventured two of them to New England, and pay the others to the right owners, I meane my creditors who may justly clayme a title to all the sugar I make so long as I am in theire debts, of which I have paid (I thanke God) neare foure hundred pounds sterling value, with the sugars I have made since the middle of February last. I pray, present my service to our Aunt Peacock and all our friends.

I am, your affectionate kinsman and servant,

CHRISTOPHER JEAFFRESON.

P.S.—Sir. I pray send me *per* the first shippe:

A demi-castor hatt which, if good, will do almost as much credit as a better in this island.

A good perrewig.

A laced cravat and cuffs.

As much broad cloth as will make me a fashionable suit ($2\frac{1}{4}$ yardes I had last).

A suiteable lining and trimming of any colour, except blew or yellow, which I now weare.

A douzaine yards at least of ribbons for cravatt and cuffs.

A fashionable and handsome belt (the last was a very good one but is decayed now).

A payer of silke, and 4 payer of thread stockings, larger and stronger than the last.

Enough silver and gold lace to lace my hatt round.

Sewing and stiching silke, white dimmety to make 2 payer of linings, and whatever else is necessary. Only skins for pocketts are not serviceable here.

8 payer of shoes, which is more, I hope,

then I shall weare out here, after the arriveall of these things, which I shall expecte about Christmasse; if sooner the better.

Yours,   C. JEAFFRESON.

LETTER XXXVIII.

[*Note.*—This letter, which bears no address, was not entered into the Letter-Book, but is preserved on a slip of loose paper, found amongst Christopher Jeaffreson's other writings. It is in his own writing, and is probably the rought draft of the epistle which he sent to his sister to inform her of the marvellous resoluteness with which the Captain General's sister-in-law had rejected his addresses. It is possible that as she was only fifteene yeares of age, the young lady (with a fortune of fifteen hundred pounds *and* four negroes) thought her suitor too old, as he had just entered his thirty-second year. J. C. J.]

St. Christopher's Island, 28 July, 1681.

About ten days ago, I advised you by a letter, by Captain Norwood, that I was bound for Nevis; whence I am lately retourned, without having had any further successe in the matter I went about, than I had when I writt. Nor can I discover whence it is that I received such a suddaine check as I did in my progresse after so fair and kind a reception, and after she had heard me several tymes with patience, showing no symtomes of dislike, nor giving any denyall, but by silence, which is more usually taken for consent. Insomuch that I doubted not my successe. Then, I say, on a suddaine, to my great astonishment, she gave me a brisque denyall, and in better language than might be expected from one of her age. I must confesse I looked upon it only as a formality until, finding her inflexible for three or four dayes (during which I was more dilligent than ordinary), I took my leave and was absent 5 or 6 weekes, but not longer, before I writ to her. My letter was received as a former had beene. But I was soon debarred this liberty allsoe on payne of having my letter returned, sealed; as my rival's was about the same tyme myne was received, whose designe was that his should have passed, under the notion of its being mine. But that intrigue, though pleasant is tedious to insert. Upon the renewing of my suit she confirmed her refusall, by reiterating of it, without showing the least cause for it. All the satisfaction I have is that I know who they are, that undermined me; and, if they have blowne me vp, they have so scurvily burned their owne fingers, that I am confident they repent of ever putting them in the fire. The gentleman, whose interest they endeavoured to advance, was the most gentill merchant, both for birth and education upon that island, and had great concernes; but he tooke strange measures in his amours, vainly boasting his interest with the young lady to be much greater than ever it was, or probably will be. And by such like indirect courses he rendered himselfe obnoxious to her relations, to whom he was never acceptable on that accompt, that, seeing no hopes remaining, he hath deserted not only his suit, but alsoe the island, and is gone for France. Thus all their endeavours to crosse my affections, and her friend's inclinations, by creating in her an antipathy against me, have not at all profited any of them, but may prove to the disadvantage of some of them. I am not at all dejected at my fate, which some would persuade me is not irrevocable; but, seeing that so it is, I must live in hope of a future successe, which I looke for in England; whence, lest I should be diverted by the apprehensions of cold weather, which I feare would be too rigid a companion at first for one that comes out of this warm clymate, I have desired the favour of you that you should once more take the trouble of cloathing me, for which purpose I have sent a catalogue of my wants in part; and, if I should be upon my voyage before they arrive, which I hope will be before Christmasse, they will not be lost, but will come to a good market. Pardon the trouble I give you not only yearly but dayly, who am &c., &c.

LETTER XXXIX.

To the Writer's sister, Madam Brett, and her husband, Charles Brett, Esq., Channell Row, Westminster.

St. Christopher's Island, 25 October, 1681.

Dear Brother and Sister. . . . . . There have happened great alterations in this and the adjacent islandes, of which I shall give you this account.

Saturday the 27th of August, about one or two in the morning, the winde blew very hard at north-east, which did some small damage. Before day, the weather broke up with appearance of fair weather; but before nine of the clocke, it was overcast and proved a rayney, blustering day. About eight or nine o'clock at night the wind, veering more to the north and from the north to the northwest, increased till midnight; at which tyme it blew so vehemently hard, and so continued with small rayne and frequent lightnings, until within less than an hour of daybreake (when the storm began to cease), that I had not a house standing upon my plantation, in which I could shelter myself from the weather.

It was a little after midnight, when a great part of the roof of my dwelling-house began to fly away; several of my out-houses being allready downe. Then I thought it time to shift for myselfe; which I did. Turning my people out before (who had been driven into my house by the insufficiency of their out houses), I locked the door, and tooke the key in my pocket.

I could not goe against the winde; and with no small difficulty could I goe with it, for feare of beeing driven away by it. At last we got (all but one of our company) to a little hut, which, we had agreed upon before, to make our rendezvous in; which sheltered vs from the violence of the storme, but not of the raine, the thatch being partly blown away. But to be wet was then no news to vs. Wee were in continual feare oure little cottage should have beene blowne away; whiche rocked like a cradle. As soone as the storme began to cease, I went up to my house whiche I found miserably torne, and flat with the ground. My sugar-worke, in like manner, and all my buildings. I walked downe to my new sugar-worke, which I had built not long before, about a quarter of a mile or more from my house, towards the sea, to make my tenant's sugar canes; to whom I had leased fifty acres of land, and had newly begun to make sugar at it, and was then boiling at it, when the storme began. I found *that* likewise flatt with the ground,—the stone wall overturned, and the timber scattered in divers places, farre distant from the house.

I must confesse, I did wonder more to see any house standing, than to see what was destroyed, considering the impetuosity of the weather. I had scarce time to view this losse, when the winde being shifted into the south, the storme began afresh. I made what diligence I could (the pathes beeing all spoyled), to gett to the place where my dwelling-honse did stand; to whiche the winde assisted me, being in my back, but veering to the south-east.

It blew a frett of winde, and continued with suche violence for severall hours, that it did much more damage in some partes of the island than the fore-part of the storme. But it was not comparable to the former with vs. I stoode for shelter behinde that part of the wall of my house, which was left standing, till I feared it would fall upon me, and then shifted to another shelter, little better than the former.

About ten or eleven of the clock, the wind ceased; but most part of the day was wet and rainy, very uncomfortable for those that had neither victuals to eat, dry cloathes to put on, or a house to shelter in, or fire to dry themselves by—which was the condition of most people. It was a deplorable sight to see the spoyle that was done in the canes and provisions, in comparison of which the losse of all our houses and workes is as nothing.

That day, although Sunday, I got up a little house, in which to secure myselfe and the best of my goods from the wet; and I used all diligence to gett up a couple of roomes, and one of my sugar-workes, and to put some Indian provisions in the ground, having thirty-two negroes, besides whites, to feed every day (for which I blesse God). I was now indifferently well at my ease for the present; my two roomes being built, and everything indifferently well in order, towardes the repaireing of my buildings and my other losses. When on Tuesday, the fourth of October, after a very tempestuous night, about breake of day, a second hurricane began, whiche lasted until two or three in the afternoone. I used all the endeavours I could to secure my new house, where I was lodged. But all my endeavours were not sufficient, but that, about ten or eleven of the clock, the roof was blown away over our heads all at once and carried many yardes from the house—and *that* in a very instant of time. But I thanke God none of vs were hurt, but one who had a small hurt with a nayle in a board.

I made what haste I could out, and passed the remainder of the storme at the side of a wall, which afforded me some small shelter. This and the other hurricane were more fierce here and in an other quarter, than in any other part of the island, as appeared by the effects of them. The damages done by this second storme, were very great, and would have beene much more, had not the great spoyle wrought by the former hurricane deprived it of matter to worke upon. Though this was not so tedious, or exceedingly fierce as that, yet it hath destroyed our provisions, and hath occasioned a sickly and scarce time amongst vs. It was most violent at Antegoa, where several ships were cast on shoar. In both stormes Montserrat hath susteyned little damage, in comparison of the other islands A New England man, bound for this island with provisions, was cast away upon that island. Captaine Cushing, master, and Captaine Clarke, from New England, having thirty or more horses on board, lost 24 or 26, as he was coming into Nevis. I had two horses on board him; one I lost, and the other, which I sent for for my owne riding, is, I thanke God, arrived safe. I am now in dayly hopes of hearing from you by the ships expected. My duty to Colonell

Gamiell, and my services to yourselves and all our friends.

   Your affectionate brother,
     CHRISTOPHER JEAFFERSON.

LETTER XL.

To the Writer's aunt, Mrs. Peacock, at Dullingham House, Cambridgeshire. Dated from St. Christopher's Island, 10 November, 1681.

Describing the effects of the hurricanes of the 27 and 28 August, and 4 October. Speaking of the damage done by the earlier storm, the writer says, "It bore downe strong stone walled houses before it, as well as trees and timber buildings. It left me not a house or sugar-worke standing on my plantation. It broke and twisted my sugar-canes, rooted up my Cassava, and washed the graine and new-planted putta-toes."

LETTER XLI.

To the same person. Dated from St. Christopher's Island' 23 December, 1681.

In answer to inquiries respecting the precise meaning of the writer's letter to his sister about Mrs. Frances Russell of Nevis. The aunt seems to have been in doubt whether her nephew was jesting or in earnest. Declining to enter into particulars, the nephew admits that he has suffered a disappointment of love, and promises to be more communicative on the matter when he shall see her in England next summer. " In the meane tyme," he observes, " I will assure you I am very well satisfied in that particular ; and, be it for losse or gaine to me, be it a misfortune or the contrary, I chearfully submit to the will of Him, who is the only wise disposer of all things."

LETTER XLII.

To the Writer's brother-in-law, Charles Brett, Esq., Channell Row, Westminster. Dated from St. Christopher's Island, 24 December, 1681.

Expressing his cordial gratitude for his brother-in-law's many services. " I thinke myselfe," says the writer, " extreamly happy in so faithfull a friend, so loving a brother, and esteeme him no lesse deare to me than if consanguinity had made the same knot that affinity hath tyed."

CHAPTER VIII.

HOMEWARD BOUND.

(12 July, 1682, to 17 September, 1682).

The 'St. Nicolas'—Tediousness of the Voyage—Mishaps in a Gale—The Writer's Accounts—Orders to his Agent and Steward—Ensign Edward Thorn—The Writer's Consideration for his Negroes and White Servants—List of his Friends in St. Christopher's Island—Their flattering Farewell to him on his Departure for England—Westcoat Bay near Margate—Off Dover—Entertainment on Board Ship—The French Success at Algiers.

LETTER XLIII.

To Ensign Edward Thorn, the Steward of the Writer's plantation in St. Christopher's Island. Dated from on Board the 'St. Nicholas,' 24 August, 1682.

[*Note.*—On leaving the Leeward Islands for England, in July, 1682, the writer entrusted Mr. Edward Thorn, now an ensign in the St. Kitt's Militia, with the management of his estate in that island. From subsequent letters it may be learnt in what way the ensign discharged the functions of steward of a valuable estate, and how he repaid his employer's confidence and liberality.—J.C.J.]

"It is this day six weekes," the writer begins, "since I parted with you, and we esteeme ourselves yet many leagues from the land, which (if the windes, now favourable, should hold soe) we may expect to see in a fortnight or ten dayes at soonest; but if the windes are contrary, as it is feared they will, it may be longer. The occasion of the tediousness of the passage has beene long calmes. For three or four dayes after we left St. Christopher's, the windes fayled vs, and for five weekes togeather, we had such gentle gales, that our ship (which is foule and requires a full sayle to carry her along) made very small runs, except it were twice or thrice, when it blowed indifferent hard, but did not last long. But we made a shift to spend our two top-masts, that is, main and fore-top masts, which sprung both at the once, one night, which hindered vs from making use of the gale, that otherwise we might have done, it being some dayes before we could get up new topmasts. During the calm weather, I improved my time by the settting of accompts in my bookes, many of which are imperfect." Of the minute and uninteresting details of the accounts, it is enough to say that they exhibit discrepancies, which at the least indicate great carelessness, on the part of the accountant, Ensign Thorn. This letter is marked as 'Not Sent.'

LETTER XLIV.

To the Writer's steward and agent in St. Christopher's Island, Ensign Edward Thorn.

[*Note.*—The opening half of this long letter is devoted to a critical examination of the accounts of the writer's plantation, and a tedious but necessary enumeration of the errors that have crept into them through Mr. Thorn's remissness. Though they do not prove a case of dishonesty, these errors demonstrate the accountant's habitual carelessness and inaccuracy in a manner that must have occasioned his employer some disagreeable apprehensions for the considerable interest committed to the negligent book-keeper.—J.C.J.]

From on board the 'St. Nicholas,' 30 August, 1682.

Ensigne Thorn.—. . . . . . I pray remember to send me the copy of my letter of Attourney as you promised; and if it please God to divert the destructive storms, let me now and then taste of my Plantation fruits, by sending me two or three barills of choice sugar, a few coquoa nutts and the like for presents. I feare the parrots I bought will not answer the ends I intended them for: they want that use of theire tongues, which should prefer them to acceptance, and are therefore scarce worth presenting. If you can procure an Antegoa parrot or two, upon any reasonable terms, send them by some Guinney ship, on board of which they are better understood, and preserved alike than in most other ships, but there is nothing like to a master of a ship that is a friend. Such like rareties may serve for a diversion, until you are in a condition to remit sugars. Be diligent and carefull and, I pray God prosper your honest endeavours. I hope your ague and fever have quite left you, and that you are by this tyme recruited. If so, blesse the Great Giver of health by improving of it to his glory, and by abstaining from those things which are the false, flattering enemies of our interest, temporall and spiritual. If Nanny's child be liveing, let it be called Valet, adding only the *t* for sound's sake to *vale*, for it was my farewell—comeing into the world just as Captain Ingle came to an anchor in the Road. Be careful over the negroes, especially the sick and weakly. Be sure to put in provisions enough; and remember that November and December are the cheife moneths in the yeare to plant Indian provisions, and to keepe the provision ground full, by planting as you dig and draw. Because when the dry weather season falls in, you will have several moneths, in which you cannot put in any provisions; which is a great prejudice to such as are neglectful. Herein I shall forbeare troubling you any more at present with these things. Only I entreat you, that your endeavours may not be wanting; that you would be as little absent from the plantation as may be. The blessing of God be upon you and me, and prosper vs in all oure undertakings. Remember my love to John Steele. This letter is prepared on board in case we should meet with a ship bound for those islands. . . . . . .

Your truely loving friend and servant,

CHRISTOPHER JEAFFERSON.

Postscript.—I pray present my most humble service to the President, Captain Pogson, Lieutenant-Colonell Crook and his brothers; to Major Elrington, Captain Crispe, Captain Rodney, and Captain Willett; to Mr. Fox and his lady, and my blessings to my god-son; my service to Mr. Vickers, Mr. Meade, Ensign Munday, Mr. Westecut, Mr. Herron, Mr. Radcliff, Mr. Dove, and particularly to Ensign Matthews. Let my commendations be tendered to all my friends and acquaintances of both sexes, with grateful acknowledgements of the honour they were pleased to doe me at my coming off; to those whose company I enjoyed to the waterside; and chiefly to those who tooke the trouble to see me on board.

LETTER XLV.

To the Writer's agent and steward in St. Christopher's Island, Ensign Edward Thorn. Accompanying the letter, dated from on board ship, 30 August, 1682.

From on board the 'St. Nicholas,' 15 Sept. 1682.

Ensign Thorn.—I had prepared this letter to you in hopes of an opportunity of sending it by some vessel bound for the Leeward Islands; and this day being in Westcoat Bay, a few miles above Margett, at anchor, waiting for the tide to passe the flatts, where severall ships passe vs, hopeing to mete with one bound for Nevis, or the neighbouring Islands, I have made this addition to reiterate my commendations to yourselfe, and all friends and acquaintances, and to let you know that we did not put in anywhere, untill we came to Dover, where we tooke in some refreshments; and, the winde being easterly, I continued aboard, promessing myselfe to be at Graves-End before this time. We lay six hours before Dover, only waiteing for a tide, where we tooke in our pilot. We made no stop in the downes. But just now the winde, whiche has beene at or neare the north-east for several dayes, forceing vs to turne up the Channel, alters, which will retard us something; though, if I had gon ashoar at Dover, I could not have been up much sooner than I now expect to be, nor so soon as we promessed ourselves, if the winde had stood at the East. It is now nine weekes or better since we parted. Yet I thanke God we wanted for nothing all our voyage except wine, which held out pretty well. We came in sight of Dover before we eat our last turkey. And we have one 'shot' now under condemnation. We have lived plentifully all the way. Only we were a little too lavish of our liquors at first; or else we had not wanted, but now we have as much too much. Norwood had a better passage. Our pilot tells vs he had been arrived this fortnight. He informs vs also that the French are masters of the mole of Allgiers, and that the Algerines have sunke all their ships in the harbour.

     I am &c., &c.,
       CHRISTOPHER JEAFFRESON.

Part III.

LONDON LETTERS.

CHAPTER I.

OLD FRIENDS AND NEW FACES.

(17 *September*, 1682, *to* 17 *October*, 1682).

London Friends—Charles Brett's Death—Mr. Penney, the London Tailor—Mrs. Penney's Revelations touching Edward Thorn—The Young Man's Victims and Knavish Tricks—Troubles of the Kidnabbers — Captain Hill— Postponement of Journeys to Cambridgeshire, Suffolk and Buckinghamshire—Aunt Parkyns's Prayers—Governor Hill's Petition for a Loan of the Writer's House in St. Christopher's Island.

LETTER I.

To Ensign Edward Thorn, the Writer's steward in St. Christopher's Island.

[*Note.*—Attention should be given to this letter, which shows that the writer had scarcely returned to London, when he had conclusive proof that he had not committed his West Indian interest to the care of a trustworthy person. The brother, whose death is noticed in the letter, was the writer's brother-in-law, Charles Brett, of whose parentage and interment in St. Margaret's Church, Westminster, mention has been made in a previous note.—J. C. J.]

London, 25 September, 1682.

I have beene now better than a weeke at London, where I found my sister a widow. My brother had beene deade sixteene weekes. I blesse God, I found the rest of my relations in good health, and all our friends. Only Mr. John Beddingfield, who dyed yesterday of small-pox, is this day to be buried. I sent your letter to Cambridge, which your mother told me yesterday is miscarried. There are several persons, much dissatisfied with the proceedings, the reflexion of which lyes so hard on me, that it is troublesome. Mr. Avery is impatient of delayes, and all I can alledge is not the least satisfaction. It is but what I expected; and to sweeten others, expectations, I turned over all that little sugar shipped with me; to Mr. Poyntz one hogshead; to Mr. Millett one; and to Mr. Brett the tierce and little barrill. And though this be taken from your shoulders and layed upon mine, who least deserves it, haveing never made the least profit of any of the goods, there is something else that has done your reputation ten tymes more prejudice than the vallew of the concerne, which is this.

By chance it happened that I had bespoke a riding coat at one Mr. Penney's, leaving directions where it should be brought. His wife, who knew that her husband was gone to the same place to enquire for one from beyond the seas, began to question me if I was no lately come from the West Indies; if I know Mr. Thorn; and so on untill she had discovered unto me, that they had sent a venter, t the valew of thirty or forty pounds, by you, which I perceive was the best part of that argo you cunningly called your owne. M. Penney was with me this morning; and not only he, but your mother and several othr friends are ashamed, and very much concerned, that you should make no better complyance with him. For my part, I can make no excuse for you. I must tell you I am heartily sorry to finde so little of conscience, so little prudence, and so little sense of honor in one that I have allways wished so well for. Who but you would have exposed his name, and had his honesty called in question for a trifle? It looke; like a loose inconsiderate slighting of your reputacion, which is the chief basis of a young man's fortune. What wisdome can it be to sell the love and esteeme of one's friends at so cheape a rate? I have apologised for you as much as I reasonably could; but I am too sensible that, as you made me believe these things were your owne, so you made use of them, and the produce of them which was considerable. I must deale plainely with you. These are great discourgements to me and my hopes; especially when I consider how closely you ordered your affaires, magnifying your little nothing and discoursing of building a store-house. I would fain know with whose money, or to putt

whose goods in? I must deale plainely with
you. I find your friends here are not in a
condition (or, if they were, are not willing)
to send you goods; so farre have you forfeited
your credit with them. I am heartily sorry,
that I should give you occasion to complaine
of the harshness of the style of this my first
letter to you. It is partly in complyance
with the request of your mother and friends;
and really I had rather give you a caution
not to build up the fabrick of your fortunes,
with the materials of others, least a storme
of justice should throw it upon your head.
It is my desire that you should live and
thrive which, with the blessing of God, I
hope you may. You shall finde me a reall
friend, if you please not to be my enemy. I
am afrayd you will see such examples made
of the selfish dealings of oure friends in
those islands, as may demonstrate to you the
folly of dishonesty. I have palliated and
excused, as much as I could, theire proceedings; but it is wonderful to see, how many
of the transactions and passages in these remote islands come to be made public on the

exchainge. Nothing is hid, and some additions are made upon small grounds, which are the offices of some people. By which means some persons here are so incensed against their agents there, that the best arguments I can use in their behalf, in which I have not been sparing, will scarce inclyne them to moderation. I thanke you for your letter by Captain Clarke, with the letter of Attourney. If you thinke you can grinde Serjeant Waugh's canes, without prejudice or hindrance to your owne, his propositions are not unreasonable; but you know it is to neither of our profits to grinde to halves, if we could have canes enough of our own. I thinke to sende you at least one servant; but, being newly come to towne, I have not heard of any servants, and you must know the kidnabbers and their employers have beene brought into such troubles, that servants are now more hard to come by than ever. I am sorry for my losses. I wish you may not be so unfortunate in horseflesh as I was in negroes; but I shall never blame you for what happens accidentally. Only let it move you to consider, how much more reason you have to be a good husband for me, especially untill my debts are payed. You doe well to settle the upper land. You must not denye leases to those that will not settle on other termes; but do not exceed seven yeares in any graunt you make. . . . . . I thinke you will not be long without a new Governour. Captain Hill, who married Madame Russell, has obteyned (or very near obteyned) the company as well as the island, and has bespoke the Great Caban in Captain Helmes his ship. But nothing is certaine under the sun. Assure all our friends, who were pleased to write by me, that their letters for this towne were all delivered with mine owne hand the first weeke after my arrival here, and those on the exchange, the same day,

Your affectionate and truely loving friend,
CHRISTOPHER JEAFFRESON.

LETTER II.

To a Country Gentleman, for whom the Writer had brought letters from the West Indies.

London, 7 October, 1682.

Sir.—It was my ambition to have been the bearer of the inclosed to your and your lady's hands, as I have come hither from the West Indies. But failing of the happiness of meeting you in towne, and my business not allowing me the leasure to have the honour of waiting upon you in the country, I was loathe to detaine your letters any longer, lest by that meanes you should miss the opportunity of answering them by Captain Bartholomew, who will saile by the middle of next weeke at the farthest; or by Captain Helmes who will not be gone this fortnight. I hope this will come safe to your hands, and if it does I begge your acceptance of my most humble service, which although a stranger I am bold on this occasion to tender to yourselfe and lady. Having nothing more to offer at the present, seeing the inclosed letters from Sir James Russell and his lady will more largely inform you, and give you better assurance of their welfares than can be received from me, whose ambition it is to have the tytle of

Your most humble and obedient servant.
CHRISTOPHER JEAFFRESON.

LETTER III.

To the Writer's steward and attorney, Mr. Percivall, of Dullingham, Cambridgeshire.

London, 7 October, 1682.

Sir.—These are, after the tender of my service and best respects to you, to acquaint you that about fifteene or twenty dayes since I arrived here, where I hope to see you as soon as your occasions invite you to London. The winter coming on, I thinke not to be at Dullingham before the spring, my business here not permitting me yet to leave the towne. There are so many yeares passed since I saw you, that I shall be covetous of your company when you are here; which I advise you of before, that you may order your affaires, so as to afford me as much of that satisfaction as possible. In the meantime I desire you would lett Mr. Fyson know of my arrival, and present my kind love and service to him and his wife. I know if I had not arrived, you would have made some retourne of my moneys hither this terme, upon which I have my great dependency, being now about to send a cargo to the West Indies, for which purpose I thinke to take up some moneys for the present. The terme now draws neare; which makes me hope it will not be long before I have the opportunity of kissing your hands, who am, Sir,

Your faithfull friend and servant,

CHRISTOPHER JEAFFRESON.

My sister Brett presents her service to you.

LETTER IV.

To the Writer's cousin, John Jeaffreson, Esq., Roushall, Clopton, Suffolk.

London, 7 October, 1682.

Dear Cousen.—Since my arrival at London, of which my sister advised you by her letter sent to you the last week, I received yours dated the twentieth of February last; which was laid aside for me here in expectation of my coming over this summer. I am glad to hear that you and yours are in good health, and I retourne you many thanks for your kinde remembrances of me. I hope, if it please God we live, I may have the happinesse to see you the next summer, when I shall be better able to give you an account of our relations, and of other particulars by word of mouth than I could doe by writing. I am sorry to hear that Mr. Matthew is fallen from his bargaine, seeing that Mr. Marshland is grown too great for that little farme, putting in his substitute and sub-tenant, whiche I feare will prove very prejudicial to that land. But for this time I shall say no more concerning those matters; but with the tender of my hearty love and service to yourselfe and all my cousens,

I remain as ever, Sir,
Your affectionate kinsman,
CHRISTOPHER JEAFFRESON.

My sister presents her love and service to you and yours.

LETTER V.

To the Writer's aunt, Madam Parkyns, of Nottinghamshire.

Honoured Aunt,—I am ashamed that I have been so negligent in paying those respects most due to you, since my arrival here. It is as contrary to what I designed, as it is to my inclinations; both which induced me to a more speedy compliance with this duty. But I have beene so hurried to and fro with one businesse or another, that I must begg your pardon; if I have let slip the occasion of presenting you with my most humble service, which I now tend with many thanks for your loving letter and courteous congratulation of my arrival in England, and also for the continuance of your prayers and good wishes, which I hope will be as effectuall for the future as I have hitherto found them, and likewise for your good inclinations to make me happy in the sight of you, for which, however satisfactory soever it would have beene to me, yet I could not have wished at to so dear a rate as the hazard of your health by a winter journey. I know it is my duty to wait upon you, of which I hope to acquit myselfe the next Spring, when I have a little better settled my business and passed over the Winter. In the meantime I entreat the excuse, remaining as ever,

Your most affectionate kinsman and servant,
CHRISTOPHER JEAFFRESON.

Postscript.—My Aunt Peacock and sister present their service to you. I pray you give all our services to Cousens Lee, Cousen Tho. Dayrell, Mr. Wilkes, and all our friends.

LETTER VI.

To the Writer's cousin, — Parkyns, Esq., of Buckinghamshire.

London, 7 October, 1682.

Dear Cousen.—I was something concerned at first that you should have received the news of my arrival here from any other hands but mine owne, which I designed to have employed that way the first opportunity. In which I was prevented by my forgetfulnesse of the daye, as well as by the forwardnesse of our friends here who gave you the advice. But I am so much more obliged to you for your kinde letter, and I thank you for your many cordiall expressions of love. I am sorry to hear that your health is impaired from what it has been, but there needed no such argument, seeing the season of the yeare, as well as the length of the way, pleaded an excuse sufficient from so great a trouble, as a journey hither would be to you, even if in perfect health. I hope, if we live until the next summer, we shall meet in Buckinghamshire, where I then designe to visit you and our friends in that neighbourhood; but really I am so afraid of the winter that I dare not think of leaving the warme city, while that lasts. For, not having been sensible of cold these seven yeares, the frosts seeme verry sharp to me now, although I have had but a small tryal of them. Last Wednesday was allotted for this worke, but I was called upon to go into the cittie, where we remembered you. Our company was your Governesse, the Alderman and his Lady, and the widow, &c.,

who all present you and my cousen your wife, with theire hearty loves and service, which I desire you both to accept from him that is, Sir,

Your affectionate kinsman and humble servant

CHRISTOPHER JEAFFRESON.

LETTER VII.

To Ensign Edward Thorn, the Writer's agent and steward in St. Christopher's Island.

Dated from London, 9 October, 1682.

Mr. Thorn is informed that the newly selected Governor of the Island and his Lady have hinted broadly to the Writer, how gladly they would accept the loan of his house on Wingfield Manor, as a residence, till they should have time to hire a suitable residence. They would like to have the Manor House for three or four months. To this suggestion, or rather this open request, the Writer has replied that he has by agreement surrendered the residence on his plantation to his steward's use, and that it rests with him to decide whether they may have their wish. "It is not," the proprietor writes, " my intent, or design to, compliment you or myself into an inconvenience, but rather to avoid it, without disobliging the Governour, who, I know, cannot be long in my house without an apparent prejudice to the plantation, by reason of the great resort to him. Now such a guest is soone received, but to be freed of him, when you desire it, cannot be effected without a disobligation, which will certainly quite annihilate the past kindness."—This letter is marked " Not sent."

309

CHAPTER II.

FRIENDLY GREETINGS AND FIRST MEETINGS.

(17 *October*, 1682, to 17 *November*, 1682).

James Phipps's Ill Health—Token-Drinking at 'The Sun' —A Family Party—Constantine Phipps and the Gray's Inn Revels—Edward Thorn's crafty Proposal—Severe Handling of the Kidnabbers—Consequent Alarm of West-Indian Merchants—The Writer's Petition for a Grant of Malefactors—Mr. Blathwait—Governor Hill— His Dependence on Sir William Stapleton—John Bed- dinfield's Death—Tokens from a Father in the West In- dies to his Sons in London—Official Men and Manners— The Writer acting for the Captain-General—Information and Gossip for His Excellency,

LETTER VIII.

To Captain James Phipps, a Planter, of St. Christopher's Island.

[*Note.*—A member of a family, conspicuous amongst the merchant-adventurers and mercantile explorers of the seventeenth century, Captain James Phipps, of St. Christopher's Island, was a first cousin of the famous Sir William Phipps, the inventor of the diving bell, and brother (of the whole blood) of Sir Constantine Phipps, who, after practising for several years with eminent success at the English bar, became Lord Chancellor of Ireland in the reign of Queen Anne. In 1682, Constantine was still a law-student; and, as we learn from this epistle, and a subsequent letter, he played a distinguished part in the Gray's Inn Revels in 1682-3. So little is known of the early stages of his career, that especial attention may be claimed for the information which the Letter Book affords us, respecting this remarkable man, who, besides attaining a high dignity in his profession, won the far brighter distinction of Dean Swift's friendship and admiration. It should be observed that, though Christopher Jeaffreson always addressed the Phippses as *his* brothers, and though their children were accustomed to style him " uncle," the relationship was only one of affinity. Sir Constantine's title

to remembrance has been strengthened by
the merit of his descendants, the Lords
Mulgrave and Marquises of Normanby, who
have in various ways shown their natural
and reasonable pride in the eminent lawyer
who was the originator of their greatness.

In the family-meeting of Phippses at the
Sun Tavern near the Exchange, to drink
Christopher's good health, on his return
from the West Indies, we have a pleasant
example of a social usage that contributed
not a little to good-fellowship in the seventeenth century. To keep himself in the
memory of his kinsmen, or friends, in a
particular neighbourhood, from which circumstances had placed him at a considerable
distance, an Englishman of that period
would take occasion to send *tokens* of undiminished friendliness to the remote circle
of acquaintances, in the form of money, to
be spent at a friendly gathering of " the
set," for " glasses all round," or a complete feast. In some cases, the bearer of
the tokens was instructed to distribute pieces
of money to the challenged comrades, and

then to summon them to the festal drinking. In other cases, he was required to lay out the token-money at his own discretion on a banquet, to which he called the selected friends with timely notice. In the present instance, Captain James Phipps furnished the money for the token-feast, sending it by the letter-writer to his brother Constantine, who invited the party and officiated as host. A letter of a later date gives us another example of this quaint and obsolete form of hospitality; the cost of the banquet, which took place in London, being defrayed by another planter living in one of the Leeward Islands.

The Lord Chief Justice, who is said to have handled the " kidnabbers" with wholesome severity, was Sir Francis Pemberton.

Mr. Blathwait was the Secretary of War, Clerk of the Privy Council, and Secretary to the Committee of Foreign Plantations, of whom John Evelyn remarks: " 18th June, 1687. I dined at Mr. Blathwait's (two miles from Hampton). This gentleman is Secretary of War, Clerk of the Council, &c.,

having raised himself by his industry from very moderate circumstances. He is a very proper, handsome person, very dextrous in business, and, besides all this, has married a great fortune. His income by the Army, Council and Secretaryship to the Committee of Foreign Plantations, brings him in above £2000 per annum." The Letter-Book affords some suggestive revelations of the means by which this more fortunate than scrupulous civil-servant raised his nominal income to so large a sum as £2000, equivalent, in Charles the Second's time, to £10,000 at the present date.—J. C. J.]

London, 15 November, 1682.

Dear Brother.—I writt to you by Captain Bartholomew, who was bound for Jamaica, and to touch at the Leeward Islands. He sailed from Gravesend about three weekes since, by which I gave you an account of my arrival here, and of the death of my brother Brett, who departed this life, the 24th of May last. I have received yours per Captain Rogers, by which you advise me of the losse of my black horse; and Ensign Thorn, by Captain Clark, writes me word of the death of my best iron-grey horse—which I hope is no more than the same; only a mistake in the colour.

I am heartily sorry to hear of your illness. I should not rejoice in seeing you upon such an occasion; but if you finde it absolutely necessary to change the air, I could wish you would not deferre it, as too many have done, until it be too late. For health is or ought to take place of all other considerations. And let me entreat you, my dear brother, to bring the summer along with you, when you come; for seriously I have found it inconvenient for me, who was in healthe, to arrive in so colde a season as I did. I presently got a great colde, which at best I feare will keepe me company this winter, though I have been and am very carefull of myselfe. It was bitter colde at my first. coming to England. Nay, we had snow with raine some tyme before we came neare the channell, and that for severall dayes.

We spent your tokens at the Sun Tavern

behinde the Exchange; where were present Mr. Jackson and his lady, Mr. Constantine Phipps, Mr. Thomas Phipps Phipps and his lady, and kinswoman, one Mr. Langford (an acquaintance of our brother Constantine) and his lady and kinswoman. Mr. Francis Phipps was in the country; and my sister, whom our brother Phipps (I thanke him) was pleased to invite in the roome of Mr. Brett, was forced to deny herselfe the happinesse of that good company; her condition, as well as dress, rendering her an unsuitable companion for vs. We dranke your health, and were freely merry. I have seen your brother since, who is pleased to call upon me sometymes, as he goes to Westminster Hall; and when I go into Holbourn, I do no lesse. He is one of the revellers of Gray's Inne where there are to be very great doings this year.

Ensign Thorn, by his last letter, has proposed something to me, wherewith I presume he hath not acquainted you nor Captain Willett, in which I could gladly advise with you both. The thing is this. Some few tenants having begun to cleare and settle above Balcony-hill, there are several (as he informes me) who would willingly rent land there at 80lb. per acre, for seven years, provided they might be secured to have their canes made to halves. Now, he offers me, in case I think not fit to be at that charge, to join with me in the expense, in expectation of halfe of the profits of the produce. Upon which I could do no lesse than congratulate his good fortune, that has put him in a condition for such undertakings, and offer him some observations, which I would have him consider before we go too far in it. For I tell him, I am loath to engage to worke for other men for seven yeares, lest it should prove a snare to draw me into trouble, who being absent may easily be condemned for breach of covenants. And at the best the profits will be small. And, though my partner's credit may be equall to mine, yet, if by accident, it should be blasted, I know who runs the hazard of paying the whole debts, whatever becomes of the plantation. Therefore, I am something backward in it, being willing that the old workes should be cleared, and put in a posture of making some returnes, before I launche forthe upon a new one. Yet I am unwilling wholly to reject the design, before I hear what your opinions are of it. Therefore I desire you would acquaint Captain Willett with it, but so that it may go no farther.

I have sent over four new coppers, and a still, and all things suitable for my upper work, with canvas ossenburgs, blew-lining, and hoes, bills, shovels, nayles, and other iron work; tarred rope, shoes, druggs, and other necessaries for my plantation and family; that new debts may not be created before the old are satisfied.

I designed to have sent more servants. But I have not yet had the leasure to make the enquiries that are now necessary on these occasions. I have had several in my eye; but, when we come to treat, they will not go on ordinary termes. And the Lord Chief Justice hath so severely handled the kidnabbers, and so encouraged all informers against them, that it is very difficult to procure any. One of the kidnabbers, a slop-seller, hath been fined five hundred pounds sterling; and Mr. Bauden and Mr. Baxter, with several eminent men, have been in some trouble on this score; and poor Captain Winter is prosecuted and put into print. To avoide which scandal, and the inconveniences attending, I am told that several eminent merchants, who have dealt to Virginia, Barbadoes and Jamaica, are glad to compound with their old friends, the kidnabbers, who, finding the sweet advantages of turning informers, Judas-like betray their masters. This is a general disincouragement to the merchant, the procurer, and the masters of ships, who are very scrupulous of how they carry over servants.

The evil consequences of this being considered by Sir Peter Colleton, Colonel Bayer, and some others, they were to wait upon the Chief Justice, who having heard their reasons, tolde them his designe was only to punish and prevent the abuses of spiriting children or persons, under age or bonds, from their parents, masters or the like.

But for such, as were of age, and at their owne disposal, and willing to transport themselves, he would never be their hindrance. But in the meanetyme, that trade hath received such a shock, that I am afraid it will not soon be settled againe; the offices, which were as conveniently as illegally set up for that purpose, being put down. Yet, however, no one thinks it worth his while to be diligent in it.

It will not be impossible to procure some; but as to the 300 malefactors, I see small hopes of them (though Captain Hill perswades himselfe, he might have had them, if he had stay'd) for the security is very large—£100; and the prison fees will be slowly paid; the prison-keepers must be well feed; and at the best they are enemies to the order, by as much as ready money is acceptable before trust. Besides they are to be had only by tens or twenties at most at a tyme; and that so seldome, that the island will not be so advantaged by it, as was expected. I would fain draw some merchants to be concerned in it, but they will not allow it to be worth their while; and I must confess there are many ways to employ money to better advantage. But this is for a public more than a private good. I have been several tymes to Mr. Blathwait, and have discoursed the businesse with him; as well this, as that of the recruits for the companies. But I received but small encouragements from him.

He hints to me, what indeed is too true —that it is an ill tyme to move or presse for anything that must be a charge to his Majestie, moneys being extreme scarce. But I designe to stir in it, and at least to prepare for a more seasonable occasion of pressing it home; if I meet not with too great discouragements, by reason that I have no grounds to goe upon, but the General Letter. Whereas you know he that appeares, being a private person, for a public interest, ought to be armed with authority and instructions from that public, as also with a fund, or else he runs the hazard of being rejected or discountenanced.

But as I have not, nor expect any of them, soe I intende to run the hazard of the consequences, in regard to which, if they fall upon me, I must be excused, having done my endeavours.

Captain Hill and his lady have taken theire passage in Captain Helmes' ship, by which I sende this. I writt you in my last, that he was going over governour, as he is; but he has no commission for it or the company from his Majestie, only the king's and duke's letters to Sir William Stapleton, which, as I understand, are not recommendatory to either government or company, but in general termes; so that his dependence is wholly upon Sir William Stapleton's kindness, and promise, made by letter, of both those places. Upon which encouragements and by the incitements of their private concernes, he goes on discoursing as if he would soon retourne, in case the islanders receive him not kindly:—*sed revocare gradum, hic labor, hoc opus est!* By that acquaintance I have with him, I

believe him to be a very honest, just, trew-hearted man, altogether a souldier . . . . . .
I remaine, deare brother, yours, in all fraternal affection, to love and serve you,

CHRISTOPHER JEAFFRESON.

LETTER IX.

To Ensign Edward Thorn, the Writer's agent and steward on St. Christopher's Island. Dated from London, 16 November, 1682.

Entering carefully into the consideration of Mr. Thorn's proposal for the management of the land above Balcony Hill; and setting forth seven arguments against the project, which, however, the writer will not decide upon finally, until he shall have further considered it.. From the first of these seven reasons against the scheme, it seems that the writer has changed his opinion respecting the policy of growing indigo. "Let us" he says "consider the extreame low rates sugar now beares, with the small likelyhood of its rising; and whether indigo, whose price dayly rises, is not like to be a better commodity. It is produced with lesse charge, made with less trouble, and with less danger of the hurricanes. Bearing two or three crops per annum, and sometimes four or five cuttings, it is my opinion it would turne to a very good account; better than sugar. Were I upon the plantation, knowing what I now know, next to the perfecting the settlements already made, I would plant indigo, the profits of which the planters understand but halfe; having it in low esteeme, only because they made but small quantities, which was all that could be expected from so few hands, as everyone then had."

LETTER X.

To John Steele, one of the Writer's white servants on St. Christopher's Island. Dated from London, 17 November, 1682.

Announcing that the writer has seen John Steele's wife, who is less happy with her relatives in England than she hoped to be, and is ready to come over to her husband in the West Indies, if he wishes to have her there.

LETTER XI.

To Captain Willett, a planter on St. Christopher's Island. Dated from London, 16 November, 1682.

Condoling with the captain on the death from small-pox of his brother-in-law, John Beddingfield, and giving the latest news of the West Indian coteries in the city of London. "I have ventured," he continues, " to make some new disbursements for the advantage of my plantation, in hope that it will repay me in tyme for all charge and trouble. I have sent out 4 coppers, a still and worme cases, and what is usual for a mill by Captain Helmes, who carries your new Governour and his lady, whom I have reason to believe you will finde an honest, just man, a true son of the Church of England, of a good courage, not proud or fantastick, but of a sociable temper and good nature. I finde that the Duke of York and Earl of Feversham are his good friends, by whom he is recommended to Sir William Stapleton."

LETTER XII.

To Captain Pogson, a planter on St. Christopher's Island.

[*Note.*—The 'tokens' were gifts of money from the captain to his sons living in the family of Mr. Wrayford, a West Indian merchant. The writer's account of his interview with official persons, is noteworthy. J. C. J.]

London, 14 November, 1682.

. . . . . I delivered the tokens to your two sons at Mr. Wrayford's, who were then both very well, and continue so. I saw Mr. Wade at the Lord Mayor's Show which, by meanes of discontent, misunderstanding and division in the city, was scarce worth seeing. Mr. Wrayford is removed into Bow Lane, and Mr. Simpkin is newly married. He and Ensign Matthews payd us their socage money at the Swan Tavern, over against the Exchange, (where we remembered you and the rest of our friends in Saint Christopher's). Yesterday I have delivered the muster-rolls to Mr. Patrick Trant, who sendes the red coats and money for the soldiers by this ship. Let it not be to my prejudice, if as a friend, I only acquainted you that upon some discourse had with Mr. Blathwait concerning our island and the recruits to be sent out, on my happening to say something of the wants there in hard tymes, by which some have been near to perish, he told me they were all payd to the last yeare. Which when I seemed to wonder at, believing it would be great news to the officers in the islands, he seemed willing to recall his words and spoke doubtfully. Now, whether it was his mistake or otherwise, I don't know. But I shall endeavour for your sakes to inform myselfe further in it, as occasion shall permitt. I cannot understand by Esquire Trant and Mr. Blathwait, that the Lords of the Committee (or I should have first said, the King and Councill) have beene ever moved for recruits for the companies. So that it will be new to them. For Esquire Trante tells me, he never received any letters from Sir William Stapleton to that effect. He asked me if we did not want money for the fort, whiche I looked upon as a flourish; the commodity being very scarce at court, as well as in the cittie, or else it would be more easie to obtain recruits then as I finde by Mr. Blathwait it is like to be at this juncture.

LETTER XIII.

To General Sir William Stapleton, Captain-General of the Leeward Islands.

[*Note.*—This letter was not entered in the Letter-Book. The incomplete draft of it, here transcribed, was made by the writer's own hand on a loose sheet of paper.

Evelyn's 'Diary' contains several allusions to Sir Robert Holmes, Governor of the Isle of Wight, and owner of "Cranbourne Lodge, in the Forest," where on 22 June 1674, he entertained superbly "his Majesty, the Queen, Duke, Duchess and all the Court," including the diarist.—J. C. J.]

(No date).

May it please your Excellency.—I made it my first business, so soone as I came to London, to deliver Your Excellency's letters and papers, which by reason of our tedious passage came not so soon to hand as might be expected by Your Excellency or was wished by me; it being neare nine weekes before we arrived at Dover, which was the first place we put in at, and the only place where our boat went ashoar; for, the winde being easterly, we came not to anchor in the Downes; though the winde, when we came into the river was not altogeather so favourable as we expected. For Captain Ingle persuaded me, when I discoursed of goeing up in the coach, that with that winde we should be sooner there by water than by land. And the difference that was, happening at the latter end of the weeke, was very little hindrance to businesse. Monday morning I came to London; and Tuesday morning I was to wait upon Mr. Blathwait with your letters and papers. It was Thursday before I met with Sir Robert Holmes, who, so soone as he had read your letter, told me he would immediately go about the business. Captain Billop, who had a much shorter passage than we (being, I suppose, conscious of what might come after him) had pressed so for his tryall that, after a little confinement in the Marshalsea, he was cleared by the commissioners of the Admiralty. But since the arrival of your Excellency's papers, the business is brought about again; and I thought it would have come to a hearing upon Saturday last before the Council. But Captain Billop got it put off; and Mr. Blathwait could not tell when it would come on againe, for that his Majesty is going to Newmarket. I left the muster rolls at Mr. Trant's, who lives now in Bloomsbury, but was not within. I have since met with him at Whitehall, where he told me he was sending over money and cloathes for the soldiers, by a vessel that goes in company with this ship, as I understood him.

END OF VOL. I.

www.ingramcontent.com/pod-product-compliance
Lightning Source LLC
Chambersburg PA
CBHW031432230426
43668CB00007B/499